Bridge for Peace

Foundation for Freedom

A Course in Deliverance

Annette M. Eckart

Bridge for Peace Publishers
Wading River, New York

Bridge for Peace Publishers PO Box 789, Wading River, NY 11792

First Printing, August 2016

Foundation for Freedom: A Course in Deliverance Copyright © 2016 by Annette M. Eckart

ISBN 978-0-9845306-4-9

Available through Bridge for Peace, PO Box 789, Wading River, NY 11792
Phone (631) 730-3982 fax (631) 730-3995 www.bridgeforpeace.org

Scriptures in this book include direct quotations, as well as the author's adaptations, from various translations of the Holy Bible.

Printed in the U. S. A.

Dedicated

to

JESUS CHRIST

Who Paid the Price

TABLE OF CONTENTS

TABLE OF CONTENTS

ACKNOWLEDGEMENTS

I am sending flowers today! In Uganda, where I have been privileged to spend a lot of time, we show appreciation by giving hand flowers. One wriggles their ten fingers, joyfully moving outstretched hands toward the recipient, while making a whooshing sound.

First, flowers to Lori Knowling for encouragement and 20 years of collaboration celebrated in the midst of the creation of *Foundation for Freedom*. Flowers for the numerous above and beyond moments! Flowers for editing, and braving the final frontier of design. You are courageous! Flowers to Kevin McKernan for wisdom, knowledge, and hours at the design board checking and rechecking the blueprints, while Karen shined the light! Flowers for the willingness to photograph tiles! Saved by the wheat! You reign as Comma King! Flowers to Kathy Bolduc for making herself available, sensitive suggestions, and lightning speed turn around. You make writing, life, and everything in it better. Flowers to Don Brisson for sharpening his pencil because God said so. Flowers to Mark Thornton for hours invested in accuracy. Flowers to Anna Sinn for sharing firsthand knowledge of Israeli customs and history. Flowers to Bill Batcher and The Scribblers with appreciation for thought-provoking questions.

Flowers to Renae Wienke for perseverance and determination and for organizing the awesome *Foundation for Freedom* pilot team in Temora and West Wyalong, Australia. Late night conference calls crackled across the Pacific, but we did it! Flowers for all it took for you to get it done. Flowers to every member of the pilot team—thank you all for pioneering. Flowers to the intercessors and to the precious members of Wednesday and Saturday Wading River B4P prayer groups where I learn so much. Thank you for your encouragement. Flowers for text messages from Sally Worner. Flowers to Lorraine Zito for cross-training. Flowers to Nina Kennedy for obeying God. Flowers to all B4P teachers worldwide as God continues to use you to reveal the meaning of His Word.

Armloads of bouquets to my beloved husband Edward. Once again, we never knew what would happen next! "Prophesy to it!" So much laughter (hilarity?) and the shared excitement of Holy Spirit set-ups refueled us. God said work while it is light, but there were nights when the light was about to rise again! We are in our purpose, love you, and every moment God gives us together.

My entire garden and everything growing there I give to Jesus Christ my Bridge for Peace.

PREFACE

For with You is the fountain of life; in Your light we see light. Psalm 36:9

I catch my breath as dawn breaks through the woods to our east and golden light shoots across our backyard gilding grass and the trunks of maple trees.

When the sun sets, a curtain is drawn over the woods. They are concealed by the darkness. Yet sometimes light wakes me in the middle of the night. Not the brilliant yellow joy of the sun, but still and startling moonlight. I have often slipped outside to stand in it and even to dance with it.

I did all I could to stand in God's light while creating Bridge for Peace *Foundation for Freedom*. Certainly there were moments when I danced with the light.

I pray Christ's light guides your study of the Bridge for Peace *Foundation for Freedom* course. I pray the purity of God's presence shines through each page with His brilliance, so multitudes sitting in darkness cannot miss the heavenly beam of hope. I pray boldly, because I know He answers with His grace, independent of my knowledge or skill.

To God be all glory for whatever you find between these pages of value. For it is by His light only that we see light.

May Holy Spirit illumination guide you through Bridge for Peace *Foundation for Freedom* and by His light may you see much more than what is written here.

Peace,
Annette M. Eckart

Wading River, New York
August 16, 2016

INTRODUCTION

Suggestions on How to Use this Course

Renae Wienke headed the pilot group in Temora, New South Wales, Australia that tested the *Foundation for Freedom* course. Renae collected the feedback and made suggestions. Participants reported stories of immediate implementation of principles presented and anointed results.

Facilitator Sharron Coleman said a young man in her group was freed in Chapter Three in the discussion of music as a spiritual weapon. "He had never sung or played in public before. He left the room and came back with his guitar. He began to sing with a voice so anointed it touched my heart and ministered to me deep in my soul."

As Gillian Bett pioneered the course she commented on Chapter Six, The Piercing Sword. She wrote, "I have noticed, just by doing the study, deliverance is happening among us spontaneously. God is really 'cleaning us up' like never before. And of course it just makes us more passionate about setting others free!"

Renae Wienke said, "A new lady was moved to emotion all night just for participating in *Foundation for Freedom*. At the end of the night she thanked us because God had done great things in her. Everyone is getting stirred by the Holy Spirit." Some of the following suggestions on how to optimize the course come from their experience.

I strongly suggest you view the DVD with the course workbook. View the first twenty minute teaching then begin the corresponding chapter. The DVD is my experience, the course workbook is yours. I recorded the DVD to help you learn from my years of listening to the Lord, studying His Word, and praying for people worldwide alongside my husband Ed and with Bridge for Peace teams. If you prefer, the course workbook can be used without the DVD and vice versa. To get the most from *Foundation for Freedom*, I urge you to do them together.

Foundation for Freedom can be used independently or with a group. There is space to record your notes, so you will not need a separate notebook. You will need the Bible(s) of your choice. If you plan to study alone, the study is divided into eight chapters. Again, I recommend you view the DVD and then delve into the accompanying chapter, working at your own pace.

Ideally, if you plan to study the course as a group, plan ten meetings. Renae worked out a schedule for her participants. Overall, they met weekly, but sometimes a break was scheduled due to holidays. The itinerary kept everyone informed of what would be covered and was a handy reference to check the meeting dates.

When several participants have never met each other, a getting-to-know-you introduction circle welcome night is a lovely way to begin. You can distribute the course workbook at that meeting. At the end of the evening view DVD Lesson One. During the week participants complete Chapter One. The next week, we suggest you form groups to discuss the questions. We have invariably found God's wisdom expressed through students. Group participation brings a rich dimension to the course. Time for personal prayer may also be appropriate while in group. At the end of the evening view Lesson Two.

God bless you as you undertake the *Foundation for Freedom* course. Enjoy your exploration of God's Word. Ponder the questions; take time to search your heart before responding. Invite the Holy Spirit, our Perfect Teacher, to guide your study. I am sure God will give you new and exciting understandings.

Chapter One

Inheritance

In her present circumstances the expected money would be a real help to Andrea, a single New Yorker. And, it would give her a nest egg for the future. She lived simply. Her only family was her brother Dean, his wife, and two children who lived half an hour away. Her sister-in-law had expensive taste and an extravagant lifestyle that Andrea knew her brother could not afford. The emotional gap widened between them as Andrea felt tolerated, but never welcomed. Their elderly father was a savvy businessman who had moved south with their mother for the warmer climate. They had both died and left an inheritance to their two children.

Dean managed the estate. After several months Andrea asked, "What's the status?"

"It's challenging," he said, "dealing with real estate at a distance and resolving problems with the business assets." Eighteen months passed. Finally, the estate was settled. He told Andrea, "There is nothing left. Don't ask any questions."

Inheritance is a proven source of blessing and cause for conflict. Time runs swiftly and legacies pass down through generations. Sometimes the transfer of wealth moves smoothly into other hands like a leaf easily deposited on the river's shore. At other times the legacy is like a branch caught in violent rapids, crashing against obstacles, stuck between boulders, and eventually eroded by legal fees in a vicious family battle. The transition may be friendly or antagonistic but, as certain as death and new life, wealth will change hands.

Houses, jewelry, and stocks will be monetarily assessed, but we have a spiritual inheritance that cannot be valued on a balance sheet. Visible in the supernatural, apparent through faith, and described for us in Scripture, our Christian inheritance impacts our daily life and our eternal reward. Do not let your inheritance fall into the wrong hands. Learn how to receive and secure this precious gift.

LACK OF KNOWLEDGE IS DANGEROUS

Like Andrea, who did not know what her inheritance contained, we have not plumbed the depths of what it means to have an inheritance in Christ. Like Andrea we wait knowing we have promises from our heavenly Father. Like Andrea we expect good from our Father God, but we are not sure exactly what our spiritual inheritance contains. Like Andrea many of us

1

never claim our portion. Others know the promises, but fail to apply the wealth of heaven deposited to our account through the Holy Spirit.

God's promises are your legacy, your inheritance. When opposition threatens our God-given inheritance, many unknowingly relinquish inherited treasure into the grasping hands of Satan. Uninformed as to our inheritance, unsure of our rights, and unschooled in how to protect them, we are vulnerable to Satan's manipulations. Meanwhile Satan, the robber, conceals the value of our legacy in Christ. Satan draws a veil of deception over our minds and delights in our ignorance.

Christ gives us truth in His Word and Satan attempts to dissuade us with cunning lies. Christ presents the authentic, Satan tempts with the glittering counterfeit. Christ invites and guides, Satan badgers. Christ remains constant and faithful, Satan changes tactics to gain ground. Christ conquered the grave, Satan threatens us with fear of death. Christ delights to give us the Kingdom, Satan rejoices in tricking us into spiritual, emotional, and physical poverty.

Slam the door in the face of the intruder. Learn what your inheritance contains. Be empowered to stand against the tide of darkness that leaves hopelessness in its wake. Discover how to be free from persistent fears and intimidation. Begin to walk in the authority of God, and through increased sensitivity to the Holy Spirit disable the strategies of Satan. Learn to become an overcomer. Help others find the ancient pathway of deliverance through Jesus Christ. Protect what is precious and God will multiply His treasures in your life as you declare to the enemy, "Access denied."

Your supernatural inheritance in Christ is the crux of the cosmic battle. From the Bible's first book of Genesis through the last book of Revelation, demonic activity focuses on robbing God's children. The ultimate goal is to strip us of the treasures won for us by Jesus Christ through His death and resurrection. God details the blessed legacy He gives us, but Satan's dark presence confuses our understanding and obscures the simplicity of God's Word. Our ignorance and disbelief in our inheritance through Christ causes us to choose wrongly. Sin is often caused by lack of understanding of the spiritual inheritance won for us through Jesus Christ. People reject God's promises through lack of knowledge of what they contain. Others familiar with God's promises fear they are not meant for them. The story is as old as Eve.

God created Adam and Eve, gave them power and authority, blessed them, and provided for them. God gave them a healthy sense of themselves. (Read Genesis 1:26-30.) All of this was given to them as an inheritance. The word "inherit" comes from *inheritance*, which means being admitted as heir. They were welcomed into the Garden of Eden as heirs and God provided for them. They had done nothing to earn it.

Chapter 1
Inheritance

A Course in Deliverance

TEMPTATION

Cunning Satan enticed Eve through the persistent suggestion that she lacked something. His tactics remind me of a course I took in college when the professor discussed the psychology of advertising. One principle used in marketing was called "create the need." The method was designed to cause people to feel and think that they needed the product. The teacher said, "People make choices based on need or greed." The point was to convince people that they had to have the item and motivate people to purchase the merchandise. If it was a luxury item, the appeal to greed was made with phrases like, "you are worth it" or "you deserve it." Every facet of an advertising campaign is scrutinized to overcome objections and get the customer to the "Yes." It's over forty years since I took the class, but advertising hasn't changed because these methods continue to prove successful. Satan used the strategy long before the existence of ad agencies.

Imagine Satan's smooth tongue suggesting Eve had an unmet need that the delicious fruit would satisfy. Of course she objected. Eve heard God say she and Adam must not eat of the tree of the knowledge of good and evil or they would die. The Devil expected that, he was not deterred. Satan anticipated her objection and methodically led her past her resistance, creating the need, leading her to the decision to act. Ultimately, Satan closed the deal. Eve must have the fruit and the wisdom it would bring her at any cost, overriding even fear of the death God said would result. (2Corinthians 11:3) Eve evaluated the forbidden tree to be good for food, delightful to the eyes. She assessed her situation through the haze of deception and agreed with Satan. She lacked something. She needed wisdom! She thought how wonderful it would be to have wisdom. Why, she would be like a god herself! She yielded her soul.

Satan makes enticing offers and many of us protest. We know immediately the suggestion is wrong. Satan is not put off, but continues with his scheme. He wants us to reason as he reasons and brings persuasive arguments calculated to overcome our objections. God's love and blessed provision keeps us from grasping the glittering offer Satan presents. The Holy Spirit shows us the true prize through Jesus Christ. While we ministered in Brazil Satan tried out his same worn routine.

Organizers of a B4P Brazil auditorium event called for a lunch break. As I left the platform a mother brought her twenty year old daughter to me. The situation looked grave, the mother's desperation obvious. The daughter had a brain tumor, blurred vision, headache, and inability to walk. Because of Jesus, her symptoms left immediately as I prayed. The mother wept; we thanked God as we went on our break.

3

Bridge for Peace Foundation for Freedom

Charles sat across from me at the table and the talk was all about people's healings. He was a translator from a local English language school. God's glorious power excited all of us as we witnessed people healed of diseases diagnosed as incurable, discouraging illnesses, and long-term disabilities. People with restricted mobility demonstrated ability and many were reconciled with God. On the B4P team, we experience and expect God's miracles because of His Word and remain in awe of healing power from the cross and resurrection of Jesus Christ. However, our translators and Brazil support team never witnessed Holy Spirit healing power as they saw it operate that morning. The translator was fascinated by the preached Word and the healings he saw happen. He told me some of the miraculous healings he saw as the B4P team prayed in Jesus name.

He said, "You are like a goddess!" I was horrified. My friend next to me gasped and barked, "No, no, no!" Charles insisted the meeting was like heaven to him, and in his eyes I presided over the meeting. I told him the Holy Spirit presided over the meeting; I was merely one of His servants. I further explained that the heavenly atmosphere was created through the unity of B4P team members who serve with love and give God all glory for every healing. When believers honor God it feels like heaven on earth.

I know he meant well, but I recognized the same dark spirit who had spoken to Eve when Satan told her she would be like a god. Satan tempts us to spiritual pride, self-glorification, and superiority. He used Charles to create and appeal to a need in me, but instead the Holy Spirit quickly showed us Charles's need! We took the opportunity to tell him about the only living God. When our joy is in God, the suggestion that we would be idolized as gods is not enticing, but repugnant. This is where Eve slipped.

Eve lost her joy when she decided there was a lack in her life. She figured God hadn't given her wisdom. Yet all the while she had direct access to God Himself Who is all wisdom. If Eve realized what she had, Satan's scheme would not have enticed her. She didn't ask God about her perceived need for wisdom, she didn't talk it over with her husband, but she rushed into a decision based on a false sense of deficiency. She wrongly assessed her inheritance in God. She decided against the Word of God and chose to get what she judged she lacked. The end was tragic.

Knowledge of your inheritance in Christ is power God wants you to have. It equips you to choose rightly in moments of temptation. (I strongly recommend you become familiar with your inheritance in Christ through my Bible course called *Foundation for Healing*.)

KEY TO UNDERSTANDING

The word "saved" is a key to our inheritance. Jesus Christ "saved" us on the basis of His mercy. Read and record the following scriptures. Notice the use of the word "saved".

A Course in Deliverance

1) Titus 3:4-7

_____

_____

_____

_____

2) Romans 10:13

_____

_____

_____

_____

3) Acts 15:11

_____

_____

_____

_____

The word translated as "saved" is the Greek word _sozo. Sozo_ means save, deliver, protect, heal, preserve, do well, be whole, make whole.

Bridge for Peace Foundation for Freedom

The Scriptures clearly show us four features of our inheritance through Jesus Christ:

- Salvation
- Healing
- Deliverance
- Provision

These scriptures tell us an inheritance belongs to those who call Jesus Christ Lord. He fought for our inheritance and triumphed. We inherit the prize—the joy of glorious new life through Christ. God blessed Adam and Eve with a healthy sense of themselves from the beginning. The Word says they were naked and not ashamed. (Genesis 2:25) They found no fault with themselves. They enjoyed healthy self-esteem until Eve listened to her enemy Satan. Satan still tells the same lie insisting, "You are not enough."

4) What kinds of temptations do we open ourselves to when we believe we are inadequate and/or that God has not given us enough in proportion to our needs?

_____

_____

_____

_____

5) What could change in you or in your life, if you believed eternal salvation, supernatural healing, the freedom of deliverance from bondage and oppression, and every provision of heaven, belonged to you as an inheritance through Jesus Christ?

_____

_____

_____

_____

Chapter 1
Inheritance

A Course in Deliverance

HOLY SPIRIT GUARDIANSHIP

My friend Lois is a bank vice-president and heads the department of wealth management. She administrates multimillion dollar trusts passed through a will or a court settlement. Sometimes the court finds someone ill-equipped to handle their own finances. Lois's department protects the individual by overseeing the management of their money. Her clients may be underage or they could be old enough legally, but immature. They may be vulnerable to unscrupulous people for various reasons. She disperses the funds according to the court's legal demands. She may pay the mortgage and living expenses for the person named in the trust.

In our case, the Holy Spirit administrates the inheritance funds we have in Jesus Christ according to the New Covenant we have through His blood. The inheritance is fully ours and the Holy Spirit teaches us how to "spend" the supernatural and material gifts God has given us. Yet the whole inheritance belongs to each person who calls Jesus Christ Lord, in the same way it legally belongs to the person who received an inheritance through the court system.

We have the fullness of our inheritance when we call Jesus Christ Lord, yet continual growth is part of God's plan for us. God counsels us to be bold, be courageous, burst free of unbelief and experience the marvels He will do through us. Our inheritance in Christ is a trust committed to us, incomparable in value, and a personal advantage in every human dilemma. God wants us to succeed. He never plans for us to fail! He has ensured our success by providing the Holy Spirit to administrate our inheritance for us, to mentor us, and to guide us into His fullness. Though God has given us an inheritance, we cannot keep it in our own strength. The Holy Spirit lives in us and guards our inheritance.

6) Write 2 Timothy 1:14

_____

_____

_____

_____

If we don't familiarize ourselves with God's promises and learn to know the Holy Spirit, Satan will gladly administrate our inheritance for us. Remember, Andrea never knew what she was entitled to through her parents' wishes and legal will. She ended up with nothing. Don't let that happen to you.

7) Andrea never knew what was in her inheritance. She left the administration of the wealth she was given in her brother's hands. Are you taking charge of your inheritance in Christ? How are you managing all He has entrusted to you?

_____

_____

_____

_____

_____

8) Is there a part of your inheritance that you have failed to claim? Do you need to make any changes in the way you have been handling your spiritual inheritance?

_____

_____

_____

_____

YOUR LEGACY

Eve, who had direct access to our all wise God, became persuaded that she did not have all she needed. Remember the four points of your inheritance: salvation, healing, deliverance, provision. This is a straightforward simplification of the incredible legacy we have through Jesus Christ to help you to remember what belongs to you. Satan wants to convince you God has failed to provide for you. The Word tells us in many places God will provide for all of our needs in every area of our lives. (Read Philippians 4:19.)

A Course in Deliverance

9) On the left side of the paper write four of your greatest needs today. On the right side write the four parts of your inheritance in Christ. How does your inheritance meet your needs?

YOUR NEEDS

YOUR INHERITANCE

_____

_____

_____

_____

_____

_____

_____

_____

HOW DO I KNOW I WILL INHERIT IT?

As we understand we have an inheritance, the next age-old question is *"How do I know I will inherit it?"* That very same question was asked by Abraham over four thousand years ago! Timelines place Abraham's birth at 2165 BC. God told Abraham He was giving him an inheritance in Genesis 12:1. Time passed and Abraham saw little evidence, from a human perspective, of how God's promises could be fulfilled. He believed God, yet Abraham agonized over his inheritance crying out, "Lord God, how shall I know that I will inherit it?"

The God of heaven answered Abraham using cultural symbols and traditions Abraham understood. (Read Genesis 15:8–21.) God spoke Abraham's language through a mysterious ceremony that is strange and confusing to us unless we have some background (See Foundation in Healing p. 11) God appeared as a smoking firepot to etch His promise of inheritance on Abraham's soul. The mysterious image would forever burn in Abraham's inner vision. He would never forget the smell of the smoke in his nostrils mingled with the odor of blood. His tormenting questions of "How?" and "When?" became like grains of sands loosed from the shore by a cleansing wave and lost in great waters, leaving certainty in their wake. All doubts were washed away. Only God's promises and Abraham's faith remained.

Imagine yourself in Abraham's place. Like him, you may be a person of faith who sometimes wonders "When?" or "How?" Let your personal questions regarding God's promises to you rise in your heart. Like Abraham we may ask, "When will I inherit?" "When will I be free?" "When will I know peace?" "When will I_____?"

10) You fill in the blank. What is it you are waiting for God to do for you?

_____

_____

_____

_____

_____

11) As Abraham scattered birds of prey, see yourself deflecting doubts sent to distract you from seeking God's response. God shows us how to defeat Satan and his insinuations that God does not keep His promises. What strategies help you to wait with faith to see God's promises fulfilled?

_____

_____

_____

_____

_____

12) Write Ephesians 1:11

_____

_____

_____

Chapter 1
Inheritance

A Course in Deliverance

_____

_____

_____

As God chose Abraham for an inheritance, He has chosen you. God gifted you to excel in your vocation, location, and generation. (Jeremiah 29:11) He provided an inheritance for you to ensure your future. God wanted you, He picked you. God chose you.

13) Write John 15:16

_____

_____

_____

_____

_____

Christ chose you, paid the price for you at the cross, and claimed you as God's possession. Imagine yourself at the grocery store where you choose something from the shelf and purchase it. You take it home, it is yours. Then someone turns up at your door and asks you to pay for your chosen item.

14) What would you do?

_____

_____

_____

_____

_____

15) Ephesians 1:3-6 says,

_____

_____

_____

_____

_____

GOD'S CHOICE IS NOT BASED ON OUR PERFORMANCE

God chose you before the creation of the world. That is a very long time ago! God was not influenced by your behavior when He chose you. You weren't even born. Many people feel they have to do something to be "good" enough for Christ. Others feel they are good people, so they don't need Christ. We have not been chosen because we are good or otherwise, but because of the goodness of God. You are His choice, as seen in Ephesians. He chose you before you did anything, before you were even born.

Satan will tempt you from two directions. Through flattery he will appeal to pride. He will suggest that you are extraordinarily capable and gifted so you don't need God or anything He has for you. Satan's second strategy is to demean you. Through accusation and condemnation, he will insist you are worthless, God would never love you or want to give you anything. While on mission I had firsthand experience of these two tactics of Satan within one hour. John asked Ed and me to minister to a tribal Queen. Only two people, John and the Chancellor, knew why prayer was needed. When I stood before her, God brought a song to my mind of David, an Old Testament King who shared her dilemma of opposition in the royal family. As the thought came and I readied myself to sing, a voice shouted in my head, "Sit down! Sit down! You're humiliating everyone! You're an embarrassment!" The experience was a bit unnerving. Despite the antagonism, even though I felt some awkwardness, I took a deep breath and began to sing. "...while enemies watch, He serves me new wine...."

As the beautiful Queen stared intently at me I saw with my spiritual eyes a bridge built between us. After the audience, driving back to our base, John was excited as he told me, "The Chancellor said you are a brilliant woman! You ministered to the Queen in front of the whole cabinet and no one knew what you were doing." The audacity of Satan angered me. Only half an hour ago he was telling me what an idiot I was. Now, he was tempting me to pride in "my brilliance." I thanked John for his kindness and encouragement, but I was unmoved

A Course in Deliverance

by the praise and immediately replied, "To God is all glory. I take no credit for anything." God is the One Who brought the song to my mind. God is the One Who gave me a voice to sing it. I burst into a song in the car and everyone joined in singing praise to Him. We were all exuberantly happy!

That is just how Satan will try to play you. First, you are worthless, and then you're the cleverest person in the world. Satan wants to keep you off balance and focused on your own performance. He wants to obscure the truth that you are God's chosen. He doesn't want you to succeed in God's purpose for your life and so he tries to convince you that either you don't need God or you are not worthy of God.

16) Based on your reading of Ephesians, knowing you have been chosen, how would you respond to thoughts of not being good enough for God? Satan may try to rob you by tempting you to believe you don't need God. How would you respond to that suggestion?

_____

_____

_____

_____

We must learn how to have victory over Satan. God gave us free access to the gift and the power of deliverance in our inheritance. We must know that Christ's triumph over the enemy through His crucifixion is now ours. Apply the victory of the cross when you are tempted. Guard what is yours by refusing to yield to Satan. When Satan comes to rob you stand firm, knowing what the Word of God promises. Rebuke Satan. When he wants to penetrate your thoughts tell him, "Access denied."

ADOPTION

The key word in Ephesians 1:4 is "chose." God chose us for adoption. The word "adopt" comes from a Latin root and means to choose. God offers us eternal life, protection, spiritual and physical nourishment. He will parent us with His perfect wisdom and love. Bridge for Peace Children's Villages in Uganda cares for children who have been orphaned. Some of our infants were abandoned, found alone in the jungle. Unaware of their peril from prowling animals, deadly disease transmitted by insects, and lack of food supply, they lay in the dark. They had no idea what they needed.

In each case, someone found the infant and carried the little one to the Bridge for Peace Children's Villages. We chose that child. We admitted that child into our home to love, feed, and clothe that particular baby. We have adopted our B4PCV children; we are their legal guardians and provide for all of their needs. They came from darkness into light without knowing their very lives were in danger.

Each of us has a similar story. Whether or not we realized our desperate need, God knew it. He saw the spirit of death that threatened us. He chose us, though we had nothing to offer Him. I have walked the adoption road with several hopeful women who all wrestled with two powerful emotions—ferocious love for the child in process of becoming a legal son or daughter, and fear that perhaps the court would fail to approve the final adoption. Love demands the hopeful parent face inner turmoil—torment for some—pressing through obstacles for the privilege of claiming the child as family.

God gifted us to excel in our vocation, location, and generation.

Yet hopeful parents continue to muster courage to initiate the process, because love yearns to connect. When an infant reaches out, curling a soft finger around a man's pinky, he smiles from his heart. A bond beyond words is created. The connection between parent and child is a forever relationship. Arguments and estrangements may occur, but the bond is never severed. Humankind stumbles along the pathway of love, making mistakes, causing pain, but God's perfect love never falters.

We stumbled and sinned. Sin tore us away from our Father God's loving arms. Through our own personal sin we were alienated from our Father like Adam and Eve, but the bond of His love was never broken. (1 John 3:1) The family resemblance remained, as He created us in His own image, and we can never find peace until we are restored to Him. (Genesis 1:27) He carefully planned our restoration, leaving nothing to chance. He attended to all of the details. Every good parent makes the best possible preparations for their children, but human beings are limited. God's love, knowledge, and resources surpass anything we could imagine. God gifted us to excel in our vocation, location, and generation. (Jeremiah 29:11) God wanted you, He picked you. God chose you.

Parents who have successfully adopted will tell you it is a very costly process. The process of adoption has never been more costly than what God Himself paid for you. God owns every resource, but what He gave for you was beyond any imaginable cost. He gave Jesus Christ, His only Son.

Jesus Christ paid a price to bring us back to God's family, to adopt us, because of the great love God has for us. God planned a way to restore you to His family through adoption. Remember; adopt means "to choose."

We have been chosen, adopted, and we have an inheritance. When like Abraham we ask the question "How do I know I will inherit it?" God reminds us of the "Yes" that shook the world and continues to reverberate in our generation, the "Yes" spoken by Jesus Christ. God answers every question through His Son Jesus Christ. Through Him we are admitted as heirs. It is Christ who became our defender in the court of adoption, Christ Who shows us who we are and what we have. It is Christ who scrutinized your adoption process and said with final authority, "It is finished."

17) Comment on the Father's plan to adopt you and the price Christ paid so you could be restored to God's family.

_____

_____

_____

_____

_____

_____

THE LANGUAGE OF THE CROSS

We cannot make sense of the ceremony Abraham passed through that solidified in his heart God's unfailing promises without some understanding of his culture. In the same way, many do not understand the language of the cross or the purpose of Jesus Christ's death. The necessity of blood for the establishment of God's New Covenant is like a foreign language to some. Scripture clarifies the necessity of Christ's death and the power of His blood that became life for us. _Foundation for Healing_ guides you through a scriptural exploration of the passion of Christ and the establishment of the New Covenant in Part One. God is just. He cannot allow sin to go unpunished. The just sentence for sinners is death. I'm a sinner, and I'm deeply grateful that Jesus died in my place. He stood before a human judge in a kangaroo court, was found guilty by a panel of liars, and died the death of a criminal on an execution stake. He was the perfect sacrifice, shedding His blood in the spirit of a sacrificial lamb slaughtered at Passover to free people from their guilt. And so He has been known as The Lamb of God, The Lamb Who was slain.

In 1941, Maximillian Kolby was in a death camp after providing shelter for refugees and hiding over 1,000 Jewish people from the Nazis. Men in Auschwitz were chosen to undergo death by starvation. He was not selected, but voluntarily took the place of a man who had a family. He was in the last group of men to remain alive enduring two brutal weeks of dehydration and starvation. Ultimately, prison guards injected him with carbolic acid, murdering him.

Bridge for Peace Foundation for Freedom

Maximillian followed in the footsteps of His Lord, voluntarily dying so that another might live. His heroic sacrifice saved the life of a man temporarily. Jesus Christ volunteered for you, went to death for you when you had no hope. He gave His life for you and if you receive the gift He purchased for you, He has saved your soul for eternity.

A B4P team prayer-walked a site of tragedy. Over two hundred people died there in a terrible accident. The beautifully worded memorial spoke of human comfort and human support to bring the families and friends of the survivors through a dark night. God's name was never mentioned. The memorial called the ground "sacred." The ground is precious as human life has been lost, but what has the power to sanctify?

We are not sanctified by what we do. We are not made holy by what we give up. Giving up the illegal use of drugs does not sanctify anyone. Jesus fasted, we too give up food as a spiritual practice, but that does not make us holy!

18) What does Hebrews 13:11-12 say makes us holy?

_____

_____

_____

_____

Notice the parallels regarding the blood sacrifice prescribed in the Old Testament to cleanse the guilty of sin. I was guilty. He substituted His life for mine. (Read Hebrews 12:22-24.) We have our names written in heaven. Because of Jesus we have an inheritance.

19) We have been studying and meditating on the language of the cross. What does Christ say to you now through His sacrifice?

_____

_____

_____

A Course in Deliverance

God gifted us to excel in our vocation, location, and generation. (Jeremiah 29:11) Jesus substituted for us, we are adopted into the family of God, we have an inheritance in Him, and our names are in His Book of Life. You are forgiven, loved, made acceptable, an heir with an eternal inheritance. Christ paid a price for your freedom. Now you make choices about your life. God's children have been made holy, but live out a process of purification. A lump of gold has impurities, but it is still gold. By Christ's blood we were made holy, still we go through purification.

20) Read Hebrews 10:14. How can you best use the freedom God has won for you and entrusted to you?

_____

_____

_____

_____

_____

There will be a final court, a Judgement Day, when God sits on a white throne and every person will be brought before Him. Through Jesus Christ, our names can be found in The Lamb's Book of Life. That book will be opened. And all will be judged by what is written in the book. We must be sure to receive Jesus Christ as our own substitute, the acceptable sacrifice, shedding His blood to satisfy the demand of the judgement against us. This is the foundation for freedom.

Continuous revelation can be ours and there is a pathway to understanding given to us by Jesus Christ through the Holy Spirit Who clarifies God's truth. The meaning and availability of our inheritance in Christ, the glory of our adoption into God's family, and the joy of the cross is explained to us by the Holy Spirit, Who guards us. He teaches us to choose rightly and leads us through the process of purification.

Before we go on, if you have not had an opportunity to tell Jesus you want Him to be the center of your life, I have included this prayer for you. Open your heart to Jesus as you pray. He is waiting for you to respond to His invitation.

COVENANT PRAYER*

Father, I come to you in the name of Jesus. I recognize that You love me and sent Your Son Jesus to remove my sin that separates me from You.

Father, I respond to Your love and repent of all my sin. Please forgive me and cleanse me by the blood of Jesus Christ.

By faith Father, I now receive forgiveness and cleansing in Jesus's name.

I thank You that Your Word says that I am now brought near to You because of the blood of Jesus Christ through which I enter blood covenant relationship with You.

I renounce the lordship of Satan over my spirit, soul (mind, thoughts, will, intellect, emotions) and body. I renounce every hold or influence of the devil in all areas of my life, including everything inherited through the generations, because the Word tells me I have a new Father and I only inherit from Him now. (Renounce specifics—unforgiveness, occult, etc.)

Lord Jesus Christ I invite You to come into my life and I submit totally to You. I ask You to be Lord of my spirit, soul (mind, thoughts, will, intellect, emotions) and my body.

By faith I confess that sin shall have no more dominion over me, because Your Spirit lives in me.

I confess that I am saved, delivered, protected, healed, preserved, doing well and made whole by the blood of Jesus Christ.

Lord Jesus, You are the baptizer in the Holy Spirit. I ask You now to baptize me with the Holy Spirit and fire. I believe by faith that when the Holy Spirit comes upon me I will receive power and tell people about You everywhere.

I believe that as I speak the Holy Spirit will give me the ability to speak in new tongues.

I pray in the name of Jesus. Amen.

*Available for download at www.bridgeforpeace.org

Chapter Two

Strongholds

Race alongside Paul and explore strongholds, prejudices, revelation, deliverance, and empowerment. We will learn crucial spiritual principles as we open the book of *Acts of the Apostles*. The words in the Bible are not just black marks on thin, gold-edged paper. They are heavy with the ballast of hope, light with freedom for souls, and fragrant with life in a world sickened by the stench of death. I write now as though I were sitting with you, telling you about Paul as I have known him through God's Word. Imagining the inner musings of Paul's mind, the high priest's motivations, and the spectrum of feelings is a way to be present to Scripture. Biblical dramatization is another way to light up a verse to show us what is hidden in our souls. Read with an appreciation for the Holy Spirit who is ready and able to transform every shadow within us into a heavenly light.

Bible verses inserted in parentheses help you locate and refer to the scripture story. You will note Saul undergoes a name change to Paul in Acts 13. We discussed the importance of a name in Foundation for Healing. Some say he changed his name after he preached to the proconsul Sergius Paulus and the leader converted. When you see the name change, realize it is the same hero of our faith.

Meet Paul at the starting line where the action begins.

During the night, Saul lay awake. He thought about his successful capture of women and men who revered that imposter Jesus Christ, followers of what they called "The Way." He had shoved the rabble into prison cells and slammed the door behind them, turning the key in the lock. He had compelled them to blaspheme, cast his vote against them, and urged the implementation of the death sentence. He recalled every step of his journeys to punish followers of "The Way," tramping through streets to purge the earth of this blight. (Acts 26:10-11)

Still, he was not satisfied. Lying awake, he conceived of a plan to show God his great love. He itched to put his thoughts into words and his words into action. Finally, birdcall signaled a new day. Saul threw off his blanket and arose before the sun. As was his habit, he prayed, offering all of his strength to God to guard His great name. As early as he dared, he trod the familiar path from his home to the high priest's gate. Bursting with zeal he banged on the door, certain the high priest would admire and approve his latest brainstorm.

19

The high priest's servant opened to Paul and shook his head. He was not surprised to see the intense young man. *I wonder just what scheme he concocted last night. He is exhausting the high priest trying to distinguish himself from the others.* In a weary voice he invited, "Come in, come in."

"Where is the high priest?"

Totally predictable. Consistently offensive.

"He's at breakfast. Have you had *yours*?"

Saul brushed past the servant, ignoring the sarcasm. He outlined his plan to the high priest to flush out followers of "The Way" in the distant city of Damascus, capture them, and force them to march to Jerusalem as his prisoners. Saul finished his tirade with an impassioned plea, "These blasphemers must be crushed."

The high priest stroked his beard, studying Saul. He saw a way to get even with Saul's teacher Gamaliel, renowned Doctor of Jewish law. The high priest's face burned with fury as he remembered how Gamaliel had humiliated him. (Acts 5:17-40)

Not too long ago the high priest had stood among the assembled court sages facing Peter the impoverished fisherman, now insolent leader of "The Way." The high priest advised the court to silence the rebel. Peter publicly defied him. He accused him of killing Jesus Christ Whom he claimed was now exalted at God's right hand as Messiah! He wanted to crush the impudent worm with a swift death sentence.

Then Gamaliel thwarted the high priest before the prestigious court. Gamaliel stood. His eloquent speech persuaded the Sanhedrin to release Peter and his cohorts. Drawing on historical experience with other rebel leaders, he counseled the court to leave the disciples alone. In time their movement would fail if it was the plan of men. Gamaliel convinced the court to release the disciples. Then Gamaliel suggested "The Way" might be from God. He crowned his argument with the warning, "If it is of God, you might even find yourselves fighting against God!" And he, the high priest, was reduced to insignificance as the court accepted Gamaliel's advice.

Now the high priest would defy Gamaliel through Saul, Gamaliel's distinguished student. Using Saul, the high priest would punish followers of "The Way." Consumed by revenge, the high priest smiled at Saul and indulged him, giving Saul the approval his teacher Gamaliel had withheld. Gamaliel's suggestion that those blasphemers could be God's agents still rankled the high priest, setting his teeth on edge. Inconceivable.

Chapter 2
Strongholds

A Course in Deliverance

And Saul felt Gamaliel's "hands-off" policy toward followers of "The Way" as a personal blow. He wondered why his teacher counseled tolerance of these blasphemers. Despite Gamaliel's warning to leave Jesus's followers alone, intolerance drove the hierarchy to devious measures. Another incident was about to explode, proving the depths of their hatred.

When Stephen, disciple of "The Way," performed wonders and miraculous signs in the name of Jesus Christ in Jerusalem, the people claimed God's grace and power flowed through him. Men from the synagogue opposed him, but their carefully crafted arguments proved inconsequential when Stephen spoke with the irresistible wisdom of the Holy Spirit. He bested the men from the synagogue and unholy passions flared. Mortified, they conspired to punish him.

In secret, the men of the synagogue instigated a plot against Stephen. They persuaded some men to bring false accusations against him saying, "We heard this man speaking blasphemous words against Moses and God." They seized him and brought him before the highest legal and judicial body among the Jews, the Sanhedrin. They lied and accused him. In response, Stephen detailed God's plan through Scripture and the Jewish people's persistent rebelliousness. Stephen used words like a hammer to crack their hardened hearts and shatter their resistance to the Holy Spirit. Concluding, he cried out, "You stubborn people…." Rejecting his final plea, his persecutors' fury raged. Like mad men, they ground their teeth. Covering their ears they screamed and rushed him, driven by murderous intentions. They hustled him out of the city and stoned him. Among the crowd, applauding their brutality, stood Saul. (Acts 6:8—8:1)

Saul opposed Gamaliel's counsel. He found a new champion in the high priest who validated the dark murderous spirit dominating Saul. (Acts 9:1-2) He procured from the high priest the coveted letters to the Damascus synagogues. They authorized him to take action. He raced home to prepare for his journey. Choosing companions for the expedition, he set out immediately. Wild with obsession, his breath hot with fervent death threats, he envisioned the obliteration of every follower of Jesus of Nazareth.

It was just another dusty, tedious journey for Saul. Vengeance drove him to push himself and his companions to endure long hours on the road to Damascus. He set the pace. As usual, his brain went into neutral with the rhythm of their steps. He barely took in his surroundings. Then a spectacular light flashed around him. Stunned, he threw up a hand to shield his eyes and fell to the ground. A voice spoke, "Saul, Saul, why are you persecuting Me?"

"Who are You, Lord?"

"I am Jesus, Whom you are persecuting." Saul was commanded to arise and enter the city where he would be told what he must do. Saul prepared to stand when another shock raced through his frame. He was blind. His companions led him to Damascus, where he remained sightless. (Acts 9:1-9) His physical blindness reflected his spiritual state.

TEACHABLE

As a Scripture student with the illustrious Gamaliel for his teacher, Saul knew God planned to send the Jews, His chosen people, a Messiah. Saul's hope was in the coming Messiah. (Acts 26:6) Saul said all Israeli tribes wait for the fulfillment of God's promise. He added his prayers to his ancestors' supplications, reminding God of His promise. Saul had the vision, but became spiritually blind to the truth appearing in the person of Jesus Christ.

How did he fail to recognize Jesus Christ as the Messiah? Saul characterized intelligence and dedication to the holy Mosaic Law. His abilities merited a respected teacher. As a Pharisee, (Philippians 3:5) Saul was a strict adherent to the most demanding branch of his religion. (Acts 26:5) He was no slacker when it came to studying and practicing his faith. Yet he failed to recognize Jesus Christ, Whose coming was foretold in the Scripture he studied. How did Saul miss it?

Three obstacles stood in Saul's way. First, he could not see past the traditional beliefs passed down through Judaism. Second, he absolutely embraced his ancestors' interpretation of Scripture. Finally, he adopted concrete guidelines of acceptable spiritual experience that closed his heart and mind.

Saul's tradition told him to expect the coming Messiah to be a man. Jesus Christ came as a man and said He was the Son of God, equal to God. (John 5:17-18) To Saul, this was blasphemy. (Mark 14:61-64)

Uneducated common people healed the sick and delivered the demonized.

Saul studied interpretations of the prophets Isaiah and Jeremiah. They said the Messiah, this man, would be a great political and military leader ushering in an era of peace. He would end hatred, suffering, and tragedy in the world. If a person claimed to be the Messiah but died before completing this mission, he was not the Messiah. Saul knew Jesus of Nazareth had not fulfilled his faith's expectations of the Messiah. Jesus brought division, not peace!

To Saul, as a Jew, the Holy Spirit was not a person with a distinct character. The Spirit of the Lord was the breath of the one God that at times came upon Israel's prophets, judges, and kings. Saul had no concept of the Holy Spirit as a person of the Godhead in the Trinity. To Saul God was one person, not three persons in one God.

"The Way" claimed a special Holy Spirit experience. They received and imparted the baptism of the Holy Spirit. And followers of "The Way" spoke in a strange language they called "tongues," claiming it came from the Holy Spirit. Through the Holy Spirit they spoke in languages they had not learned. This was outside of Jewish experience and therefore suspect. Many Jews rejected Peter's interpretation of Joel 3, "In the last days, the Lord declares, I shall pour out My Spirit..." (Acts 2:14-21). They expected God would pour out His Spirit, but not in that way. Saul had no faith background to substantiate this religious experience as coming from God. Many followers of "The Way" were uneducated common people who healed the sick and delivered the demonized through the power of the Holy Spirit in the name of Jesus Christ. This was entirely outside of Saul's accepted religious experience and expectations.

Saul thought he had been defending God from a cult called "The Way." Saul was a top student, knowledgeable about the Scripture and the prophets. He was very bright, but he was also very wrong. Saul—passionate, sincere, and self-sacrificing—thought his zeal came from heaven, but it came from hell. He breathed murderous threats, consumed by spirits of hatred. Unknowingly, he was a pawn of Satan used to accomplish Satan's desire, the destruction of Christians.

He couldn't see it. He had no awareness of it. Saul's self-righteousness drove him to persecute Jesus's disciples. Beliefs passed down to Saul through his faith tradition, interpretation of Scripture, and guidelines of acceptable spiritual experiences did not open him to "The Way" until he encountered an unexplainable light and heard the voice of Jesus Christ.

1) What do you think may have made Gamaliel's response to "The Way" different from Saul's reaction?

_____

_____

_____

_____

_____

_____

2) We thank God for Bible scholars and all those who have invested themselves to unlock God's Word for us. At the same time, we pray for deliverance from any way we have adopted as absolute truth a half-truth or a lie. We can be as sincere and passionate as Saul was, but be confused by certain traditions, interpretations of Scripture, and expectations of religious experience. We don't want to miss anything God has for us. Compose a prayer asking God to expose any false teachings you have believed (including messages in your culture and in the media) and asking for His enlightenment.

_____

_____

_____

_____

_____

CHANGE IN PLANS

Saul had described himself as advancing in Judaism beyond many of his own age, and extremely zealous for the traditions of his fathers. (Galatians 1:14) But when he met Jesus, his pride in his excellent theological credentials died in a moment. It was as if the papers of authorization he clutched in his hand were incinerated by the flash of Christ light on the road. He had no interest in piecing together the scattered ashes of what had been his pressing, immediate plans. His brilliant future as an intelligent and well-connected Jew, born with the desired status of a Roman citizen, became nothing to him. Temptation often follows God's invitation, but Saul grabbed hold of God's "change in plans."

Many believers today share Saul's story of a "change in plans." My husband Ed worked for an international corporation that moved south and wanted him to accompany them. But he heard God whisper "change in plans." Ed had received the Holy Spirit and been empowered to obey Christ. He did not follow the corporation out of state. God gave no details on economic support other than "Trust Me." This is similar to how God led Saul. He gave Ed a vision for B4P, but no specifics as to how it would happen. Today, B4P has led over one hundred missions and has worldwide bases bringing healing to the nations through Jesus Christ. In addition, B4P Children's Villages shelter children orphaned in Uganda. Then God added B4P RaphaEl Medical Missions to the B4P family, adding surgical/medical volunteers.

Saul grabbed hold of God's "change in plans."

3) When did God ask you to change your plans? Did you experience temptations? Did you overcome them? What helped you make the change?

_____

_____

_____

A Course in Deliverance

_____

_____

_____

CHANGE OF HEART

Sometimes a "change in plans" is coupled with a change in heart. When Christ asked, "Why are you persecuting Me?" Saul did not make a single excuse for his behavior. He demonstrated a B4P principle, "Repent enthusiastically." I admire Saul's quick change of heart.

An awareness of sin, the opportunity to repent, and the certainty of God's forgiveness is a gift that confirms He is at work in us. Satan will never encourage us to repent and be forgiven of our sin. The fact that we know we have sinned and need to ask God's forgiveness is reason to celebrate! God-in-us causes us to be sorry for sin and determine not to sin again. His mercy assures us He forgives us when we ask. Grace is God's power causing us to recognize our sin, ask for forgiveness, receive it from God, and be changed. Obviously, God's power lived in Saul! He was not a hypocrite. He didn't self-protect or make excuses.

"Repent enthusiastically."

On the road to Damascus a light flashed all around him and Saul fell down. It was not only Saul who bowed down, but the murderous, vengeful, demonic spirits that drove him also bowed down. The Devil knew who Jesus was before Saul had a clue. Jesus spoke, Saul asked who He was. Christ identified Himself and Saul's ears and heart opened. When Saul stood again, he stood as a free man, delivered by a holy encounter with the risen Christ. He became convinced Jesus Christ was Lord.

4) What does the Word say in Philippians 2:9-11?

_____

_____

_____

_____

_____

5) God sent a believer named Ananias to pray for Saul. (Read Acts 9:1-22.) What did Ananias say and do? What was the result of his prayer?

_____

_____

_____

_____

_____

As God sent Ananias to Saul, He may put your needs on someone's heart right now. Christ Himself is making intercession for you. Saul made a new choice and because of Christ we are free to do the same.

6) Reading Saul's story transmits grace, because it is the Word of God. As every force in heaven and earth bows to Christ in this graced moment, we are freed from dark influences to choose anew. What choice does Christ invite you to make today?

_____

_____

_____

_____

_____

EQUIPPING

Jesus sent Ananias to Saul to ensure he was equipped through receiving the Holy Spirit. Christ insisted His apostles received Holy Spirit power before they ministered in the authority of His name.

A Course in Deliverance

After His resurrection, Jesus Christ reminded His disciples of the gift He had already spoken of, the gift His Father promised, the baptism of the Holy Spirit. They seemed preoccupied. With the resurrection of Messiah, the apostles' dreams of Israeli political authority came alive again. Their minds buzzed with questions and they wanted answers. Jesus's interest lay elsewhere. He hikes up Mt. Olivet with them to disclose how He will equip them for worldwide ministry.

He speaks His last words and rises in the air! A heavenly cloud robes Him and conceals Him. While the disciples scan the heavens, two men dressed in white robes appear and ask, "Why are you standing there looking up at the sky?" Clearly, it was time to act on Christ's important last words.

7) What last instructions did Christ give to His followers? (Read Acts 1:3-5, 8)

_____

_____

_____

_____

_____

The disciples went back to the city, to the upper room. They waited, praying with their community.

8) What happened? (Read Acts 2:1-4.)

_____

_____

_____

_____

_____

9) Christ's last words were about receiving heavenly power. Why do you think Christ focused on His disciples receiving power in His very last moments with them?

_____

_____

_____

_____

_____

The foundation for freedom is Jesus Christ. The shedding of His blood at the crucifixion, His triumph over death in His resurrection, and His enthronement at the right hand of His Father in Heaven won our freedom from demonic powers. Christ equipped us to deliver others through the baptism of the Holy Spirit.

THE BATTLEFIELD

Saul unsuspectingly joined Satan in the spiritual battle against the followers of "The Way." Saul thought he was doing well, on a good course, headed for honor and prestige among his people, the chosen people. Saul never suspected a murderous spirit manipulated him.

Saul was the battlefield. He could not accept Jesus Christ as the Messiah because a fortress of prejudice had been constructed in his own brilliant mind. The stronghold in his thoughts was built brick by brick. Saul knew his encounter with Christ on the road to Damascus yielded miraculous results. He realized the enormity of Satan's plan to rob his inheritance. He acknowledged the uselessness of worldly weapons to free him from the bondage of his mindset. There was no human power great enough.

After receiving the Holy Spirit, Paul wages war against spirits of darkness. He exposes the strategies of the enemy and teaches us how to defeat him. Paul emphasizes our need for pulling down strongholds. He instructs us from personal experience, as he had known strongholds in his life.

10) How does Paul describe strongholds? How would you describe a stronghold? What does Paul say about our spiritual weapons? (Read 2Corinthians 10:4)

_____

_____

_____

_____

_____

Both Paul and Ananias faced strongholds that had to be overcome by supernatural power. They had mindsets directly opposed to Christ's call on their lives. Without the freedom of deliverance, neither would have fulfilled their destiny.

Paul hated the followers of "The Way." He was nearby when Stephen summarized history from Abraham to the present, authoritatively quoting Scripture, highlighting riveting scenes when some of God's chosen people rejected, refused, and resisted the Holy Spirit. (Acts 7) Still, Paul burned with hatred for Jesus Christ and His followers. His mindset was a stronghold.

Jesus told Ananias to go to Paul. Ananias had a vision of the Lord. Immediately he knew Christ had something for him to accomplish. I imagine that when God called Ananias's name he gasped, "Here I am, Lord!"

He heard the Lord say, "Get ready. Go to Straight Street."

Ananias took notes. _Got that. Off on a mission. Okay, I know where Straight Street is._

The Lord continued, "At the house of Judas…"

Judas, Judas, yes I think I know him.

"… Ask for a man from Tarsus named Saul."

Ananias froze. _Saul from Tarsus? The brothers warned me that murderer was headed this way from Jerusalem._

The Lord continued. "Saul is praying. I have shown him a vision of you coming to him. I've told him your name, Ananias. He has seen you place hands on him in the vision so he might see again."

Ananias wasn't sure how to say this, but he knew he had to jog God's memory about this Saul of Tarsus. After all, the King of the Universe kept very busy, so He must have overlooked a few facts. Ananias plunged in. "Lord, many people have told me about this man. He has done _terrible_ things to Your people in Jerusalem." Then to bring the Lord up to date he said,

"And he has come to Damascus with authority from the chief priest to arrest all of us who worship You!"

The Lord replied, "Go."

Ananias's shoulders slumped. He could see God was unaffected by his impassioned plea.

"I have chosen Saul to serve Me and to make My name known to the Gentiles."

To Gentiles! Why, they aren't the chosen people! They are idolaters! Ananias's head spun.

11) Christ exposed strongholds in Ananias's mind. What do you notice about his mindset? Could this stronghold have interfered with Ananias's purpose? How? What lesson can you draw from this?

_____

_____

_____

_____

_____

_____

_____

The Holy Spirit frees us from prejudices fostered by our family line, culture, faith traditions, etc. Sometimes we have been pre-judged and accepted those judgements as reality, harboring harmful and limiting thoughts toward ourselves. Some biases target people from specific nations, in particular career fields, or with certain economic status. God freed Ananias and Paul from prejudice.

12) Do you sense the Holy Spirit wants to free you from a stronghold today? There is no pressure to disclose private issues in your group. If you choose, discuss this question

generally to examine demonic strongholds that imprison people today and the mighty power of the Holy Spirit that destroys ungodly mindsets.

_____

_____

_____

_____

13) What spiritual weapons combat prejudice and foster community? What spiritual weapons free captives to bring hope to the despairing?

_____

_____

_____

_____

God wants to train up courageous Spirit-filled people like Ananias. I imagine Ananias felt intimidated to bring God's message to Paul, because the Devil made sure Ananias heard frightening things about him. God freed Ananias from strongholds and strengthened him to minister to his former enemy, Paul. I thank God who empowered Ananias to obey. He ministered to Paul and we have received the blessing. Ananias ministered to the man who braved perilous journeys to broadcast salvation through Christ, wrote numerous letters included in the New Testament, and left us a legacy of inspiration.

God wants His message to penetrate the hearts of people feared by the world. We need Holy Spirit power to reach all people according to Christ's expressed will. As He sent Ananias, Jesus Christ sends us to pray for others to receive the Holy Spirit.

14) Are you intimidated by a person or people group? Has Satan built a stronghold in your mind concerning them? Think it over. God wants to use you in a mighty way and Satan will try to block God's purpose for you as he tried to derail Ananias. Can you pray for that person or group now?

_____

_____

_____

_____

_____

15) Where do you see a need for spiritual power in your life?

_____

_____

_____

_____

_____

PREJUDICE AGAINST THE EXISTENCE OF SATAN AND THE BAPTISM OF THE HOLY SPIRIT

A pastor invited B4P to teach on healing through Jesus Christ in the daytime and conduct an evening service of healing prayer. During the session I explained how demonic spirits use people to satisfy cravings and perverted desires. After the session, the Pastor said he didn't believe in the Devil, the demonic realm was superstition invented to control people.

That night, the B4P team began with testimonies. The Holy Spirit surprised me as each team member shared their experience of being delivered from demonic influence.

Joan said she was always extremely self-conscious, timid, and seriously depressed. "If there were papers on the front pew in church and I wanted to get one, I couldn't walk up there in front of people." After receiving prayer for deliverance from oppressive spirits she became free, and proved it as she spoke in public.

Rhonda testified to an informal B4P discussion when we had talked about our expectations in the healing ministry. She said, "I never expected anything to happen when I prayed for someone." Listening to her, I remembered that day and how the Holy Spirit began moving me toward her. I didn't know why at the time. She began to feel nauseous and sensed the presence of a dark spirit. "Annette, get it out," she cried. We prayed and she began to gag. I took her to the sink, "That's all right, just let God do it." (Sometimes, demonic spirits want to scare us to keep us in bondage. She didn't vomit, but she was willing to do anything she had to do.) She was delivered from a lying spirit through the authority of Jesus Christ as we prayed. She now travels the world praying for the sick, and many have been healed and delivered as the Holy Spirit works through her, including a child with a life-threatening brain tumor.

John had an alcohol addiction. He said, "I enjoyed thinking about alcohol. When I was at work, I would think about when I could have my next drink." He was instantaneously delivered by Jesus Christ. "I immediately lost all desire for drinking."

Then we prayed for people to be delivered through Jesus Christ. The Pastor was my prayer partner, observing and agreeing. I said, "In the name of Jesus, as His servant, I enforce the authority of His blood shed on the cross and the resurrection power of the Holy Spirit." Immediately spirits of arthritis, spirits of pain, spirits of blasphemy, and spirits of scrupulosity left. Crooked fingers straightened out before our eyes, people stood and kicked their legs—pain free. Persistent blasphemous voices were silenced. And the torturing spirit that told a young man he was constantly offending God, no matter what he did, left for good! He testified to me many years later of his freedom from that spirit and the terrible anxiety it caused. I prayed for people to receive the Holy Spirit and each one began to speak in tongues. The rest of the team gave glowing reports of how God had set so many captives free that night.

Later, the Pastor spoke to me. "I need what all of those people received tonight." The team placed their hands on him, and we prayed. He was delivered of doubt, the fear of death, and discouragement. He received the baptism of the Holy Spirit and testified to newness of life that began that night. Through the demonstration of Christ's power over the Devil he was delivered from strongholds and received the baptism of the Holy Spirit in one day.

Remember the testimony shared above of how the Devil lied to Rhonda, now used mightily in ministry. The Devil wants to trick you into believing you are ineffective. Expect results when you pray, but know you are God's deliverer even if you don't see immediate change. Know who you are based on what God says. Do not "judge" your "success" by circumstances. In B4P our standard of success is obedience to God. The name of Jesus Christ and the power of His blood is always effective.

Bridge for Peace Foundation for Freedom

Prayer for Deliverance from Strongholds

Father, I praise you for Your Son Jesus Christ my Savior. Thank You for Your Word that says I have the mind of Christ. (1Corinthians 2:16)Thank You for those You have sent me to teach me about You. I ask You to reveal any stronghold in my life. Thank You for showing me any place I have mis-interpreted the meaning of Your Word. Thank You for revealing any "tra-dition of man" that interferes with Your Word in my life. Thank You for delivering me from any stronghold in my mind, especially the stronghold of _____. This stronghold is based on a lie. I reject the lie and Satan the liar.

I rely on You, Holy Spirit, and not on my past experience. Thank You for freeing me from any inappropriate reliance on my experience that inter-feres with my dependence on You. Thank You Jesus for washing me clean by your blood. Thank You Holy Spirit for teaching me. Thank You for deliv-ering me from any stronghold in my mind, especially_____. Thank You for showing me the truth. I pray in the name of Jesus Christ. Amen.

Chapter Three

Take the Snake By the Tail

anger threatened the newborn boy. Murderers hunted him, but his resourceful mother preserved her son's life with a daring plan. The infant gurgled as she kissed his forehead, placed him in a handmade basket covered with pitch, and pushed the baby boat into the Nile River's current. He cooed throughout the adventure, unaware of the risk. His bold mother succeeded, her son escaped the deadly plot. The chase begun in his infancy to destroy his destiny, would pursue him throughout his lifetime.

Champion of the persecuted, he took a bold stand to free the oppressed ethnic group in his nation. He fell from favor, lost political power, and fled to a backwater where wanted men found new identities.

His voice, once sure and strong, faltered. He stuttered and fell silent. Unwilling to speak, he soon convinced himself he was unable to speak. He lost his sense of purpose and surrendered his future to obscurity. For a time, darkness celebrated victory, but hell had forgotten he was born of a praying mother with powerful faith. His legacy laid hold of him.

Reluctantly, he chose rightly and found direction at a crucial moment. Stumbling forward, he claimed his inheritance. His destiny as liberator of a nation would not be handed to him. He would learn to fight, to confront evil with faith. A prince by Divine choice, he had become invisible in society, until he found unexplored courage within himself through hardship. He forged a path for a nation to follow. Under the tutelage of a Holy God, he remembered his inheritance, took hold of the promise he was born to, and rose to greatness. His name was Moses.

DELIVERANCE AND DESTINY

If Pharaoh's plot to end Moses's life in his infancy had succeeded, a great liberator would never have fulfilled his destiny. (Read Exodus 1:8-2:10.) Just as a wicked plan opposed Moses, evil raged against Jesus Christ. King Herod ruled Israel when Jesus Christ was born. Jesus Christ was destined to be the ultimate emancipator, to free humankind from death through His cross. (John 10:10) Herod's counselors advised him that the King of the Jews, their Messiah, had been born in Bethlehem. Herod raged, his reign was threatened. Determined to eliminate his problem, he repeated Pharaoh's pattern. Driven by the same demonic spirits that had possessed Pharaoh, he attempted to annihilate the Messiah by massacring all male infants in Bethlehem. These heads of state were puppets, manipulated by dark spiritual forces. The cunning spirits used the rulers' fear, pride, and ambition to advance hell's plans.

1) Compare the events of Moses's birth to the circumstances surrounding Jesus's birth. (Read Matt 2:1-16.) What similarities do you notice?

_____

_____

_____

_____

_____

2) Where do you see enormous destruction of life today? Are heads of state involved? How do/can you participate in the spiritual battle?

_____

_____

_____

_____

_____

Famous Moses, named in the Book, portrayed in movies, destined for greatness. Though Moses saw himself as unable and said he was unwilling, God was undaunted. God saw greatness in Moses. And He sees greatness in you. He put it there. He created you for His purpose and the purposes of God are never trivial. God has an amazing plan for your life and now is the time to believe.

A Course in Deliverance

3) Read Jeremiah 29:11 and write the scripture below replacing the word "you" with your name.

_____

_____

_____

_____

God is not the only one with a plan for your life. You will have to fight some battles to fulfill your destiny. You have probably had victories in your life already, but perhaps you did not realize the spiritual significance of the events. Remember, Satan plotted to silence Moses and he cooperated. He diminished himself, doubted his capacities for change, and did everything he could to dissuade God from choosing him.

4) How have you responded to voices both internal and external that attempt to discourage you?

_____

_____

_____

_____

Negative self-talk is one of the Devil's great weapons. The Word tells us that as we think of ourselves, those thoughts mold our behavior and our becoming. (Proverbs 23:7a) God knew how to lead Moses through his negativity and God shepherds us through Moses's story. Let your imagination bring Moses to the center of our study as we prayerfully accompany him. Hear the herd bleating, feel the rocky terrain beneath your feet, and the blustery wind stinging your face as we climb Mt. Sinai.

DISCOVER STRENGTH

Moses shrugs, adjusts his cloak, and squints at the shrub ahead. *"Yes, it is burning!"* His imagination stirs and he speaks to himself on the lonely trail saying, *"I will now turn aside and see this great sight. How can it be that the bush has not burned?"* He draws closer until the leaping flames reflect in the black pupils of his eyes.

Moses notes the unusual and pays attention. His turning toward the bush caused him to turn to God in a new way. But the flames in Moses's eyes did not spring from a fire in his heart. They were merely reflected glory, an image of what he saw in the bush. However, Moses took a first step. His journey would kindle a love in him that would consume every hindrance.

5) What do you need to turn toward or away from to allow God to stoke His fire in you? Remember as you answer these questions, this is your time to explore choices. Your answer may be the beginning of a work of the Holy Spirit in you as you turn your attention toward the question. Spend time to poke around a bit and see what God may break open for you. Don't get stuck on giving the perfect answer or resolving a lifelong question. Rather, begin to investigate an inner suspicion or explore a possibility with holy curiosity, just as Moses turned toward the burning bush.

_____

_____

_____

_____

_____

God calls from the bush, "Moses, Moses." Moses buries his face in his cloak, afraid to look, but it is too late for that. Moses has already seen and knows he has been seen. God assigns Moses a tough job, an unprecedented job. God commands Moses to confront the most powerful man in the world, a man who considers himself to be a god. God wants Moses to enter Pharaoh's courts not as the imperious Prince he had once been, but as His servant. There is no prototype for how Moses could accomplish it. There is no "how to" book written to guide his way, no mentor to follow. But God had measured Moses. His humility was a prime factor in his preparedness for the job.

A Course in Deliverance

Since Moses had lost all confidence in himself, he was ripe for placing his trust in God. God said Moses was ready to return to Pharaoh, the most celebrated ruler of the Egyptian Empire. God knew Moses would have to confront the strongholds he had built in his mind about himself. Moses allowed his failures to form his self-image. His current image of himself as incapable was as false as his former grandiose self-assessment when he lived as a Prince in Egypt. Moses would have to search his soul to find the truth of who he was. God was about to lead him through the process of self-discovery demanded of every servant of God who desires to be used by Him. God was about to begin His training program to free Moses from his illusions. Notice how God prepares Moses for his mission.

Though Moses saw himself as unable and said he was unwilling, God was undaunted.

Distressed by the enormity of his assignment, Moses asks God for a bit of reassurance, some solid affirmation, at least a little comfort. After all, God told Moses He would release His terrifying power. Moses has seen signs in the Egyptian court performed by Pharaoh's sorcerers. A sign from the God called I AM would be very welcome now. God tells Moses to throw down his staff. Moses's eyes light up with expectancy and he gladly complies. His stick hits the ground with a thud. Moses's lips begin to curl in anticipation of a miracle that will show Pharaoh who is boss. He fixes his eyes on the ground. The wood starts to wriggle, then writhe! Horrified, Moses jumps back and side steps. His staff, his protection from snakes, becomes a snake! This is not the reassurance he hoped for. *"What is this I Am God thinking?"* Then God says, "Put out your hand and grab it by the tail." (Read Exodus 4:1-5.)

An Australian raised in the countryside instructed me in snake handling with a story from her childhood. She and her pals caught poisonous snakes for fun and profit. They scoured her farm, checked underneath her porch and searched favorite serpent hideouts previously discovered in the paddock. "Taking hold of a snake we plunked it into a big barrel." Finally, when they figured they had all the reptiles available for one day, they got down to business. Hooking a snake, they grabbed the back of its head and milked the venom from it drop by drop. They sold the liquid to an anti-venom processor to help victims of potentially deadly snake bites. Kids must have their pocket money!

The lesson for us city folk is obvious. No one in his right mind picks up a snake by the tail, especially a poisonous snake. It will swing its head around and sink its fangs into you.

Picture Moses caught between a treacherous snake and a flaming bush. What is a shepherd to do? If he fails to grab the snake will a whirling fireball explode from the bush and incinerate him? Moses recognizes that the power of I Am speaking from the bush is greater than the power of the snake and most certainly greater than his own power. Obedience to I Am in the bush appears to be his best option. He tenses his shoulders, clenches his teeth. His work-worn hand grabs the undulating tail. The reptile twists, fixing his narrowed eyes on him with intent. Moses shudders, clutches the snaky skin, and feels familiar wood in his hand. The snake turned back into his staff.

That night, lying alone in the wilderness, the experience plays through Moses's mind like a movie. He sees himself seize the snake's tail and congratulates himself. Actually, he didn't know he had that kind of courage, but God knew. I AM pressed Moses to the moment of self-discovery. In his days as a prince in Egypt Moses had possessed a brash courage, but as years passed his bravado teetered as if on the edge of a grave and about to fall in and be buried. God brought Moses's courage to the surface through the trial. When Moses stretched out his hand, he discovered nerve he thought he had lost. He began the process of overcoming his fears. He found the strength he needed for the journey ahead.

MEET RISISTANCE WITH CONFIDENCE IN THE LORD

We look for comfort from God, but God looks for courage in us. We must overcome our fear of the "snake" in our lives. Take the snake by the tail because God commands it. We so easily miss the point and try to sidestep issues that lay before us. We recoil from situations that demand confrontation. Others of us let our fears drive us to aggression and turn us into bullies.

Stop looking for comfort and start looking for strength.

Moses sought comfort, but God gave Him self-knowledge. God wanted Moses to find the conviction he needed to follow Him. Like Moses, we must overcome fear of the powers of darkness and find courage. Face your fears. Stop looking for comfort and start looking for strength. In 2016, when Ed and I taught in Tanzania for the first time, we found we had to take the snake by the tail.

Seventy-five students gathered thirsting for sound scriptural teaching on healing. They drank in the material we presented from the Bridge for Peace *Foundation for Healing* course, understanding spiritual principles for the first time.

On the morning of the second day it was time for practical application of the scriptural teaching. We asked for people with intense back pain to come forward for healing prayer. We would demonstrate how to lay hands on them for healing in the name of Jesus. Three people responded.

Sam had a frozen shoulder. His motion was extremely limited. He could not raise his hand above ten degrees. His situation was not what we wanted to teach at the moment, but he sat in the chair and he wasn't going to move. Another woman in her late forties, Dahlia, hobbled up to us when she walked. And a third woman also in her late forties, Genevieve, had intense, debilitating hip pain and struggled to climb stairs.

A Course in Deliverance

God had trained us to pray for people in public. He wanted everyone to see what His power did for them. Jesus had made it clear that He wanted us to pray as He had in Matthew 3:1-6. "Jesus said to the man with the crippled hand, 'Stand here where we can see you.'" (MSG Bible) We had to learn to take that "snake" by the tail.

Many times people want us to pray in a back corner away from everyone. Sometimes the host group feels it is inappropriate to demonstrate Christ's power for whatever reason and can object to our praying up front. I used to worry that the person with an infirmity might feel on display and ill at ease, but God made it clear that His will must be my biggest concern. Trainees asked to come up front sometimes worry, "What if nothing happens?" Of course, if one is not expecting any improvement, praying in the back corner may be more comfortable! And Satan is ready to tell you healing will not happen.

We had to take that snake by the tail a long time ago and resist people's opinions. In obedience to Jesus Christ, we make healing a very public ministry so God receives glory.

The three in need of healing waited before the seventy-two remaining students. Our translator, Dr. Alex, explained what would happen in Swahili. Ed would minister to Sam, and then I would minister to the women. Other than husbands and wives ministering to each other, it is our practice in B4P that men pray with men and women with women whenever possible.

As Ed prayed, Sam had no visible improvement for the first few minutes. Ed continued to take authority in the name of Jesus and command the arm to be healed. After five minutes or so, Sam could raise his arm higher. In B4P, we want the person who came for prayer to tell us the change. Even if we see a change we don't lead the person. We wait until they see it for themselves. Sam did not see any change, though the increased mobility was obvious to Ed and me. Dr. Alex said, "Let's see how he is tomorrow." Ed and I looked at each other. We weren't satisfied but, when possible, we submit to our host. "Okay," Ed said. "We seal this healing in the blood of Jesus Christ and give Him all the glory." Sam went back to his seat.

Dahlia limped forward with terrible pain in her feet. I got down on my knees and prayed commanding the pain to go in the name of Jesus. After some time, she had some relief. I stood to lay hands on her hips, expecting the rest of her healing to come from that area. As I prayed, she winced. "It's in my shoulder." I glanced at Ed, because we knew exactly what was happening. The Devil wanted to rob God's glory and was stubbornly resisting. "How are your feet and hips?" I asked. "Better," she said then winced again. "Oh, it's in my knee." Experience had taught me exactly what was happening. The demonic spirits wanted to put on a show. They wanted people's attention. They wanted God's glory. As I prayed for her, she began to experience sharp pains in areas that had been pain free! In other words, she got worse.

41

Bridge for Peace Foundation for Freedom

Demons often intensify the situation. I call this "death throes." The demon knows he's going, and he acts up on the way out. God wants us to draw on the faith He's given us in these situations and take the snake by the tail. When we see this happening, we often start laughing. We can't help ourselves, the Devil is so ridiculous. That generally confuses our hosts who are getting nervous because they put on a big rally and when the healing team prays people get worse! And Ed and I think it's funny. The hosts don't think it's a laughing matter. But our confidence is in the Lord and I think God expresses His laughter through us. Psalm 37:13 says, "The Lord laughs at the wicked, for He sees that their own day (of defeat) is coming." (Amplified Bible) God knows Satan is defeated and Satan knows it, too. The issue here is do *we* know Satan is defeated. Knowledge is power.

I said to the people, "This is just demons. They want to challenge us. But they are not challenging us; they are challenging the Most High." If we don't throw down our egos before God, we can find ourselves in a power struggle with the Devil. We are not the healers or deliverers, but we are servants of the Most High, equipped and empowered as instruments of His power for His glory. Dahlia had some improvement before she walked away. Dr. Alex was very happy. Dahlia was no longer painfully wobbling along. Ed and I praised God for the obvious progress, but we were alert. Our assessment was that demonic spirits were used to exerting their authority here.

Finally, Genevieve came forward. Many students had crowded around to get a close view of what was happening. When I began to pray over her hips and prayed for the healing of any trauma due to childbirth, she let out a howl. Her back arched and she fell panting into the chair. I said to the students, "This is the Devil and he is going now. We don't have to yell or shout." I said this purposely, because the Devil thrives on noise and chaos. I wanted to prevent panic or any dramatic reaction among the students that would satisfy the Devil's craving to disrupt the class. I had to take control by instructing the class, while being sensitive to Charity's needs. Ed and I had been through the process of submission to God to conquer our own uneasiness in these situations years ago. We know what it is to look for God's comfort and find He wants us to discover His courage in us. Before God sent us to teach others we had already grabbed that snake by the tail in the name of Jesus. I calmly and quietly repeated, "In the name of Jesus and the authority of His cross get out now." Finally, she collapsed into the chair. With her eyes still closed, Genevieve said, "There are many women here who need this ministry." She expressed an awareness of emotional healing. I said, "Okay, but God is focusing on you now." That's another possible snake. Before the deliverance is complete, one could turn attention to the needs of others. Don't get thrown off course. The Holy Spirit is in charge of the session. Stay with one person until the Holy Spirit releases you. We prayed. She was totally freed from pain. Later she testified in Swahili. Genevieve said, "*Tuk, tuk, tuk, tuk, tuk...*" The students shouted with joy. I asked her daughter to translate for me. "My mom's describing how she tested her ability to walk up the stairs. She simply and easily walked up and her shoes sounded like *tuk, tuk, tuk, tuk, tuk...* as she climbed the steps!"

Chapter 3
Take the Snake by the Tail

A Course in Deliverance

We were told a person had been brought to us from the hospital. We called her forward. My translator said the lady had a dislocated foot. She was in excruciating pain and couldn't put any weight on the foot. She couldn't even bear to put the sole of her foot on the floor because of the tremendous pain. As she sat, she had her knee somehow supported on the chair and this foot dangled from her ankle. She couldn't feel or move her toes. We prayed in the name of Jesus and the feeling returned, then she wriggled her toes. Then she could put her foot on the floor. Then she could stand. She still had some pain in standing, but nothing like what she had formerly experienced. Then she walked with a slight limp, not bearing full weight on the foot. From the baseline of not being able to even put her foot on the floor because of the pain, the improvement was miraculous. Praise Jesus Christ who put down Satan's resistance. God had the last laugh and the healing flow had begun. Later that afternoon, Dr. Alex told us, "Dahlia is improving! She's walking even better!" Dahlia herself came up to me grinning, "The pain is much less." Still, Ed and I wanted to see our God exalted in public.

The next day we began the healing rally. Sam, who had the frozen shoulder, got up, testifying in Swahili to his *total* healing, giving glory to God. Then he ran across the field swinging both arms high into the air. (You can see him on our Bridge for Peace You Tube or Vimeo Station.) Dahlia testified she was totally healed. Genevieve testified again to how she could easily maneuver up the stairs.

The Tanzanian healing team Ed and I trained with Dr. Alex, who translated, ministered at the rally every day while we stood back. Miracles of all kinds flowed. Besides physical healing, people testified to spiritual healing. One young woman in her early twenties testified how she always wanted to read the Bible at night, but became drowsy and couldn't comprehend anything. After prayer she could read the Bible into the night with understanding. A tall dignified lady came forward to testify that her grandson, who had been abducted years before, had been returned to the family. Dr. Alex said in all of the years they had been holding rallies they had never seen so many healings take place. Deliverance had to come first. God had taken Ed and me through many confronting experiences in which we had to obey Him in order to walk in His authority. Taking the snake by the tail is never easy, but it brings amazing rewards.

6) When have you been in a difficult situation, sought comfort from God, and felt that the situation intensified?

_____

_____

_____

_____

7) Looking back on the experience, how did it weaken or strengthen you? If it has affected your present circumstances, explain how.

_____

_____

_____

_____

_____

God transformed Moses through his obedience into His instrument. Passionate for God, he was no longer a mere observer of the fiery bush. Flames visible in Moses's eyes were not reflected glory, but arose from his God-serving soul. He became a flame that shed light for captives groping in the dark for the path of deliverance. (Read Exodus 3:1-3)

8) After prayerful self-assessment, what will help you to go forward in God's plan for your life? Is God urging you to take a snake by the tail? Take note of your need and take time to pray for yourself right now. Write your prayer here.

_____

_____

_____

_____

_____

9) God encourages us through Moses to submit our worries and inadequacies to Him and allow Him to have victory through our weakness. Is God inviting you to submit to Him? Moses

threw down his staff signifying his work and his protection. What might you throw down before God as an act of worship and acknowledgment of God's sovereignty in your life?

_____

_____

_____

_____

_____

_____

MASTER YOUR WILLPOWER TO SEE GOD'S POWER

The human will has enormous power. When Moses saw the snake at his feet, his instinct told him to bolt. God told him to stay. He made a decision, overrode his natural inclination, and used his willpower. He had to exert his will to do what God commanded. Moses controlled his emotions by his willpower and bent down to the snake by his willpower. If Moses had refused to bend his willpower to God's will, God could not have used him. Many times we have to force ourselves to take the next step of obedience to overcome fear, destroy false self-images and, at times, conquer overdeveloped instincts of self-preservation. Go forward into freedom or shrink back and cower in the corner of a prison cell as Satan's captive. Who would know the name of Moses if he had shrunk back? His name appears 828 times in the Bible because he used his willpower to obey God. Four words from my book *Holy Chutzpah* repeat in my mind, "No guts, no story."

Nadine, a woman in Uganda told me her story. She worked in a hospital stocking the supply closets. One day God told her, "Go to Ward A. I have a surprise for you." Arriving, she found two men weeping, holding a baby girl in their arms. The mother had died in childbirth. The doctor asked if there was a woman in the men's village who could nurse the baby. They shook their heads. When they saw Nadine, they asked her to take the baby. God said, "This is the gift I have for you." Nadine was very poor, "I didn't even have a teaspoon of sugar in my house." God told her to take a cup from her home and ask for milk from a mother in the maternity ward. Nadine became very ill with dysentery and truly wanted to die. As she sat on the bed in her room, she had a vision. It was as though a movie projector cast the image on her wall. A huge angel spoke to her. "You want to die?" "Yes," she answered thinking maybe the angel came to take her to heaven. "This is your book." The angel held up a gold-bound volume and swiftly flipped through it. "All of the pages are empty. Are you sure you want to die?" Terrified, Nadine shook her head no. "What did you learn in Sunday school?" the angel asked. "To love my neighbor as myself." "That is your neighbor," the angel pointed to the baby. She now cares for 100 orphans, each day is a miracle.

In a counseling session, a struggling mother of five said, "Annette, sometimes I feel so frustrated that it takes all of my willpower not to slam the dishes down on the table." God knows the snakes of anger, discouragement, and self-pity that we struggle with. Don't let fear control your willpower. Use your willpower to act despite your fears. When we determine to follow God with our entire will we discover God has given us courage!

10) Jesus steeled Himself, exerting all of His willpower to do what God required of Him. (Luke 9:51) Recall a time when you decided whether or not to master your willpower to see God's power. What happened? What insights have you gained?

_____

_____

_____

_____

_____

_____

Consider the impact of power released by a group of people. We have an example of mutual determination in Scripture verses about the Tower of Babel. (Genesis 11:1-9)

The people planned to build a city tower called a ziggurat, considered a boundary breaker between heaven and earth. Ziggurats looked like tall pyramids with steps to a pagan temple on the top. Men got together and built towers to demonstrate their own importance. The townsmen acknowledged constructing the Tower of Babel was an enormous goal, but they determined to work together and make personal sacrifices to build the ziggurat.

God said because they joined their willpower together nothing would be beyond them, including the attainment of wicked goals. Imagine how God could use us, if we mastered our willpower and determined to use it to obey God. What if we resolved as Christians to study God's Word together, praying to the Holy Spirit for guidance, with the goal of discovering how to live in Christian unity with one another as Christ desires?

Chapter 3
Take the Snake by the Tail

A Course in Deliverance

Pride motivates human beings to work to reach the heights of heaven on our own terms. God says if we will submit to His Word, His promises will manifest in our lives. God says, "If you have something against your brother leave your gift at the altar..." (Matthew 5:23-24) But Christians worship at their various altars on Sunday morning without concern about the malice held against brothers in the church across the street. 1 John 4:20-21 says, "...whoever does not love their brother and their sister whom they have seen cannot love God whom they have not seen. And He has given us this command: Anyone who loves God must also love their brother and sister." (NIV) Christians with condemnation in our hearts against brothers and sisters in Christ violate both of these commands and imagine we will be blessed. Satan lulls us into accepting disunity as "normal" thereby robbing us of exerting our willpower to establish what God wants.

Jesus Christ prays for us who have come to believe in Him. He prays that all of us may be one, so that the world may be convinced that the Father has sent the Son. He prays for us to mature in oneness, to be of one heart and mind, to be the evidence in a godless world that Jesus Christ is Lord. (John 17:20-23)

Yet strongholds of self-righteousness, contempt for one another, and pride riddle the Christian community. As the B4P interdenominational ministry, we know the judgement, disdain, and dismissive attitudes one Christian brother can harbor toward another. Snakes of criticism and gossip slither too freely through the church. Who of us will bend down and grab them by the tail? When we command our wills to work for God's will, the miraculous will occur for us as it did for Moses. We will see that threat transformed by the power of God. It will become powerless as the supremacy of Christ manifests itself through us.

I began a conversation with two young men from India. They knew a lot about Christianity and under the circumstances of our meeting I assumed they were Christians. I asked if they knew about the baptism of the Holy Spirit. They told me they were Hindus. They asked me, "Why is it, if you Christians serve one God, you can't agree with each other?"

We reject division as "normal." When what we consider "normal" is against God's expressed will, we must exert willpower in godly obedience. Work for change and watch for miracles.

11) What submission do you see is needed to join our willpower to God's power to pick up the poisonous snake of disunity and disarm Satan?

_____

_____

_____

Chapter Four

Authority

Power questions must have rolled around Moses's brain. I AM was picking a fight with Pharaoh the all-powerful. Pharaoh's subjects obeyed or he executed them. Brutality ensured obedience. Moses had seen Pharaoh's power first hand, but had limited experience of I AM. Power counts in a battle. Moses believed God, that's why he obeyed. Still Moses most likely grappled with fear as he prepared to confront Pharaoh.

God sent Aaron, Moses's brother, to accompany Moses in the fight for Israelite liberation. Together they would confront Pharaoh. God told Moses Pharaoh would respond by asking for a miracle. God instructed Moses to tell Aaron to throw his staff down before Pharaoh and it would become a snake. (Exodus 7:8 - 10)

Moses knew God had the authority to transform the staff. His experience with the staff becoming a serpent had left a sharp impression in his mind. The brothers trudged across the desert and into Pharaoh's court where slaves and kingdom dignitaries awaited Pharaoh's pleasure. As God instructed, the brothers delivered God's message. Aaron threw down the staff; it became a snake and wriggled across the floor. Women gasped. Men's eyes widened. Pharaoh leaned forward in his seat. His eyes narrowed and he clenched his hand into a fist.

Pharaoh was obsessed with power. He kept a crew of sorcerers close at hand. They preserved Egypt's magical texts filled with curses and spells. They worshiped the demonic and pledged themselves to serve false gods. Pharaoh demanded their immediate presence.

Imagine Pharaoh's messenger bursting through the door of the magicians' domain where they made talismans and brewed potions. He urges them, "Quickly! Pharaoh wants you." While they grab for their staffs of authority, the messenger fills them in on Pharaoh's furious reaction to his unexpected visitors. He waves his hands wildly, "Moses is back!"

Thirty of them rush down the corridor, robes billowing as they hurry to the court. They babble incantations and call on demonic spirits, confident in their fiendish powers. Reaching the Great Hall, they skid to a halt and enter at a dignified pace. Ah, there are the intruders. Glaring at Moses and Aaron, they size up the situation. Smirking, they throw down all of their staffs and they become snakes.

Bridge for Peace Foundation for Freedom

The palace floor writhes. Hissing echoes through the throne room with maddening effect. Snakes seem to hang from the ceiling. Men cover their ears. Fear keeps them spinning, watching for snakes to avert disaster. As always, sorcerers who release demonic power are helpless when the dark force turns against them. In the midst of chaos, Moses's snake raises its head. Its jaws stretch open. It darts around the room by God's power, devouring all other reptiles. Question settled. No contest. God reigns.

I taught on this Exodus passage at the New Dawn Conference in Uganda. Eight thousand people attended. I sensed God's electrifying power surrounding us as we delved into the Scripture. A man sitting on the ground close to the platform jumped up and shouted his story to my translator. He had seen a snake by the river and killed it. Another snake came and twisted itself around the dead snake. He killed that one as well. At that moment, a persistent fear entered him and overwhelmed him. When he heard the teaching, he understood God's message in Exodus was for him today. He was freed of paralyzing fear. God's Word has power for deliverance now.

1) Fear startles us into awareness to keep us safe. But there is another side of fear. Satan uses fear as a weapon. Comment on your experience of fear.

_____

_____

_____

_____

_____

_____

At the same New Dawn conference, a woman came to the platform to testify. She said, "I killed a snake." From that time on a snake appeared to her every night and spoke. He said, "You killed my wife." The spirit terrorized her. Her mind was being affected. The B4P team prayed for her. She collapsed. After the team commanded the harassing spirit to leave her in the name of Jesus, she testified to a sense of inner peace and freedom.

Demonic spirits often take the shape of snakes. They terrify people in dreams and in other types of unnatural appearances. Moses's snake devouring the sorcerers' snakes teaches us

A Course in Deliverance

our God reigns over demonic power. This truth relieved many who said, "We no longer need to fear the powers of darkness for our God is greater."

In Australia a worship leader named Jacob had struggled for months as his voice had become very hoarse and had lost power. Doctors had no explanation. When a condition cannot be diagnosed, I become attentive. I have often found there is a spiritual root in conditions that defy diagnoses. He asked for prayer. As I prayed, Jacob saw by his spiritual vision a snake wrapped around his neck. I commanded it to go in the authority of the name of Jesus and the power of His cross. I asked Jacob, "What's happening?" He replied, "The snake said, 'I have to go.' and left!" Jacob cleared his throat and found his voice totally restored through Jesus Christ.

Sometimes Satan launches a series of attacks against us. Life can feel like we are tiptoeing through a dangerous snake zone. But our God has destroyed the enemy's plans. Satan cannot succeed when we understand two realities. First, all authority and power belong to our God. He demonstrated His supremacy in Pharaoh's court over 3,000 years ago and still proves it today. Second, Scripture defines our responsibilities regarding deliverance.

Scripture defines our responsibilities regarding deliverance.

The kingdom of God is not a matter of talk but of power. (1Corinthians 4:20) You are called to be the Rod of God. His instrument is not a stick of wood, but His servant filled with Holy Spirit power. We received Christ's authority to trample on snakes and to overcome the enemy. (Luke 10:19) Following Christ's pattern, we learn to cast out unclean spirits. (Luke 4:36)

2) Scripture proclamation is not idle chatter. Christ commanded deliverance and people were freed. What did Jesus do and how did He do it in Luke 4:35-36?

_____

_____

_____

_____

AUTHORITY AND POWER

Authority is the right to give orders. Power enforces obedience. God has unlimited authority and unlimited power. However, He chooses not to "take" authority over us, but allows us to

51

Chapter 4
Authority

choose to come "under" His authority. When we ask Jesus Christ to be the Lord of our lives, we ask Him to take authority over us. God established rules and empowers us to follow them.

We become citizens of heaven. We receive His protection as subjects in His Kingdom. (John 17:14-16) We are still in this world, but no longer of it. Though we live in the world we do not wage war as the world does. We have divine power which is contrary to worldly power. Christ's great power is rooted in love. (2Corinthians 10:3)

The Greek word "exousia" is used for God's authority. "Exousia" means mastery, jurisdiction, and liberty. He gives mastery, jurisdiction, and liberty to his disciples to cast out devils and to cure diseases. (Luke 9:1)

To cast out devils means to eject them, expel them, to drive them out, to send them away. The Devil cannot cast the Holy Spirit out of anyone. His authority is limited. His power is limited. We have a great advantage through knowledge of God's Word. God is greater and His power in us is greater than Satan's control over people, animals, and the earth. (1John 4:4)

3) What does God say about total authority? (Read Matthew 28:18 and Titus 2:15)

_____

_____

_____

_____

_____

We are children of God with authority to protect our territory from bullying spirits.

The United States government has authority over its borders. Official laws govern what can and cannot be done. The authority of the US government is limited by geographical areas and other factors. The US has authority to establish laws against murder. Even though these laws exist, the US did not have the power to stop the tragedy of 9/11. The authority and power of governments are limited.

A Course in Deliverance

A parent has authority over their own child, but not their neighbor's children. However, if a child deceives their parent and abuses drugs, we often see a tormented parent powerless to stop the child's behavior. The parent's authority and power are limited.

The Devil has authority and power. Because of our sin, we have given him authority on the earth. Jesus, Prince of Peace, says Satan is the "prince of this world." When we refuse to repent, fail to forgive others, or act contrary to the authoritative Word of God, we give Satan authority over us. He starts to make the rules. He abuses, pressures, and imprisons those under his power compelling them to participate in addictive and self-destructive behaviors.

4) Read John 12:31, 14:30, 16:11. Put these scriptures into your own words.

_____

_____

_____

_____

_____

_____

Calling Jesus Lord, we reject Satan and his authority. We submit to the authority of God, to God's rules. By rejecting Satan's authority we understand he no longer has the right to order us around. Satan will keep at you, like a bully. Remember, you are a child of God. You have an inheritance through Christ's cross of deliverance.

What does a child do when faced with a bully? As God's adopted child you can do the same. Say to the Devil, "Leave me alone. I'll tell my Daddy God and He'll fix you!" That's right. Remind the Devil that he has no authority over you. Command the Devil, "Go away or I'll tell my big brother Jesus that you are bothering me!" We are children of God with authority to protect our territory from bullying spirits.

There are many ways to deal with evil spirits. Learn from Michael the Archangel. He calmly called on God. (Read Jude verse 9.) Paul told us what to do. He counsels us to refuse to yield territory. (Read Ephesians 6:13) Note James's advice of humility, submission to God, and resistance. (Read James 4:6-7) Study the Master's way. Jesus's disciples gathered around Him and He taught them how to deal with the Devil. He commanded the demon to come out and go away. (Read Mark 9:25-26.)

5) Choose one of the four scripture references mentioned above regarding how to deal with evil spirits. Which scripture did you find particularly enlightening, affirming, or encouraging? Why?

_____

_____

_____

_____

_____

_____

TERRITORIAL SPIRITS

God arranged angels in hierarchies. Angels include seraphim, cherubim, thrones, dominions, virtues, powers, archangels, principalities, and angels. (Colossians 1:16) There are also hierarchies of evil spirits.

Paul refers to Satan's chain of command when he mentions principalities and powers in Ephesians 6:12. "Principalities" comes from the Greek *archer* meaning "first in order and rank." "Power" in Greek means "exercised strength." Higher ranking evil spirits command subordinates to enforce the evil principalities' commands. Yet Christ reigns over all spirit and flesh, even the rebellious principalities and powers. (Colossians 2:10) Though evil spirits are under Satan's rule Christ is head of all, whether obedient or disobedient. He has ultimate authority and power, but permits choice. Satan majors in threats, harassment, and compulsions.

As for us, we are in a wrestling match. Paul hands us the program naming our opponents. Read about the challengers in Ephesians 6:12. You and I are wrestling against principalities, powers, rulers of darkness, and spiritual hosts of wickedness. Some of these evil spirits are more powerful than others. Evil territorial spirits command lesser demons.

An angel visited Daniel and told him how it works. Daniel had been praying for days when an angel, his eyes like blazing fire and his body glittering like a gemstone, appeared to him in answer to his prayer. The angel had sprung into action immediately, but had been delayed as he battled an evil spirit, the prince of the Persian kingdom. The angel called in Michael, a chief angel, to help him fight off the prince of Persia. The angel says he left Michael the archangel contending with the prince of the kingdom of Persia. After speaking with Daniel, the angel would reenter combat against the prince of Persia and told Daniel the prince of Greece was coming. Evil territorial spirits will take charge of particular geographical areas if we do not oppose them with the authority and power of Jesus Christ. (Daniel 10:5-20)

6) Comment on Daniel's experience.

_____

_____

_____

_____

_____

7) Recall a time when God answered your prayer as you requested, but the answer was delayed. What happened? What have you found to be helpful when praying and waiting?

_____

_____

_____

_____

_____

A B4P missionary team ministered in Jamaica, West Indies. We quickly learned marijuana addictions plagued the area. We opposed the addictive spirits, praying and commanding them to go throughout our week of B4P ministry. We often sang, "We want to see Jesus lifted high, a banner that flies across this land. So all men might see the truth and know He is the way to heaven...."

Bridge for Peace Foundation for Freedom

On Saturday night, Audrey and Sharon, B4P missionaries, ministered to a woman whose husband was addicted. He never came to church. She hoped he would start attending. They prayed with her. The next day, we had a healing prayer service after church. I had preached and was sitting in the choir pew facing into the sanctuary enjoying the beautiful sight of B4P missionaries ministering to the people. Audrey came up to me and said, "The lady we prayed for last night, her husband is here! Would you pray for him?"

"Sure," I said. We approached the seated man and I asked if he would like prayer. I smelled strong alcohol on his breath. We prayed the Covenant Prayer with him. He repented, committed himself to Jesus, and we prayed for him to receive the baptism of the Holy Spirit. The aftermath of the ministry made a lifelong impression on me.

After ministering to him, I went back to the choir pews and began to feel a very slight queasiness. I could have easily dismissed it, but what I knew about deliverance ministry told me not to ignore the feeling. I walked to the back of the church where Ed, my brother Kevin, and my sister-in-law Karen had finished up ministering. "I think you had better pray for me," I said. I thought I might have picked up a transferred spirit. A transferred spirit goes from one person to another. As soon as they placed their hands on me, I sunk to the floorboards. They got down on their knees beside me and commanded the evil spirit to go.

I could hear them, but their voices were distant background sound to another voice. The voice in my head said, "I'm not leaving Jamaica. I'm not leaving Jamaica." I saw a huge yellow snake in my spiritual vision. Its thick scaly body flew like a flag over the island of Jamaica. I felt the yellow snake's jaws clamped on my throat. My family kept praying, but the yellow snake's voice was more distinct until my brother Kevin stated, "The blood of Jesus. The blood, the blood, the blood." As he declared the authority of Jesus and the power of His blood, the yellow snake was silenced. Very reluctantly it began to loosen its jaws. Clearly he didn't want to submit, but I could feel him weakening. I gave the feedback to my family and they all began to pray, "The blood." Resentfully, the snake faded.

That afternoon I shared my experience with Brother Anthony, our host and director of the retreat house. He was a native of Jamaica and understood the culture. Brother Anthony said, "In Jamaica, they call marijuana the yellow snake."

The yellow snake was flying in the sky like a national flag. When a nation is conquered, the invading enemy will swiftly raise its flag as a sign of dominion. The yellow snake spirit, the marijuana spirit, declared sovereignty over Jamaica. I had a glimpse into the spiritual realm and saw the territorial spirit. This was not a transferred spirit that moves from person to person, but evil of high rank. After ministry we always bind the transference of spirits and retaliatory spirits. Retaliatory spirits are sent for retribution. You have authority over them and it is up to you to take that authority in the name of Jesus Christ.

A Course in Deliverance

God was using us to deliver, not only individuals, but a nation. That is big. God is looking for simple people to say yes. He will use you for very big things to exalt His name.

Let's review the scenario for purposes of learning. First, we like men to minister to men and women to women when possible.

Second, at that time I could not easily tell when someone was inebriated. God has sharpened me in that area. The fact that he reeked with alcohol in the morning was a clue to the depth of the power of addictive spirits over him.

My husband and my brother are more discerning concerning spirits of alcoholism, but they were both occupied at the moment. Now when the same situation arises, I wait for one of them to be free to minister to men who are drunk. Be alert and wise when ministering to anyone under the influence of drugs or alcohol. Be sure to seek a partner to stand with you whenever possible. If you are at all uncomfortable, excuse yourself and get someone else to minister. Never violate the inner voice of the Holy Spirit.

Third, I was excited God had brought him to church. What an amazing and immediate answer to prayer. From that place of excitement one can underestimate the situation. Always put the blood of Jesus between you and the person you are ministering to. At times when someone tells me their problem, I get a sense they may say something that could be damaging. I call on Jesus and His blood to come between us and filter every harmful word or spirit.

I've been operating in deliverance ministry since 1986 and I'm still learning. If we are willing, God is able. Since this incident I have prayed with people under the influence of drugs and alcohol and God glorifies His name. I have no negative effects. Be reassured and confident in God. God has already destroyed the work of the Devil at the cross. Our responsibility is to enforce Christ's finished work by speaking the truth and evicting tormenting spirits.

8) What have you noticed or learned from my experience?

_____

_____

_____

_____

_____

Bridge for Peace Foundation for Freedom

The yellow snake was a territorial spirit, an evil spirit of high rank. A territorial spirit orders lesser spirits. Because we declared in song we would see Jesus lifted high over Jamaica, B4P took authority over the spirit of marijuana in the name of Jesus through the power of Christ's cross. We sang, "Every prayer a powerful weapon. Strongholds come tumbling down...." Then we gave a victory shout of praise. God has taught us many times the musicians and worshippers go into battle first. I am certain none of us fully realized why the Holy Spirit led us to sing "We Want to See Jesus Lifted High" as our mission theme song. Not one of us imagined what God was doing as we sang over and over again. Music is a weapon God put in us. God's people's lives depended on their songs of praise. (2Chronicles 20:21-22)

The enemy outnumbered King Jehoshaphat's warriors. The king prayed to God and said, "We have no might to stand against this great company that is coming against us." (AMP) God said the king didn't have to fight the battle. He told King Jehoshaphat to stand still and see the deliverance of the Lord. Musicians led the army that day. When music and praise went up to God, the Lord set ambushes for their enemies and they were self-slaughtered.

The enemy uses music as a weapon, also. Several young people have told me they felt "something enter them" when listening to "heavy metal music." The stories had commonalities. Listening to the music was the beginning of a downward spiral in their lives including abusing drugs, criminal activity, and destructive relationships. Parents have asked for prayers for their children who have been "lost" to them. The first step in their decline was listening to music that exalts immorality and even blasphemes God.

The prayer of music and song overcomes darkness. B4P team in Kenya worshipped on a platform supported by 50 gallon steel barrels during Ramadan. Spiritual forces of darkness opposed the ministry, but God reigns. A Muslim woman was sick in her home. She heard the music praising Jesus Christ. She was healed and came down to the rally to tell everyone!

Incorporate holy music into your personal life and prayer services whenever possible. In Jamaica we had a team member with a resonant speaking voice. I asked her to speak out scriptural words of healing and deliverance during the service interspersed with singing. The Word glorifies God, spurs on the prayer ministers, and delivers the captive.

9) Music is a spiritual weapon at your disposal. How can you introduce holy music into your life? If you already benefit from holy music, is there a new way you might use the spiritual weapon of music in your circle of influence?

_____

_____

A Course in Deliverance

_____

_____

_____

_____

CULTIVATING AN AWARENESS OF GOD

"I tell everybody you people saved my life," Pastor Teresa said. We met in China on a mission that was not lead by B4P. She and my brother Kevin had both become dangerously ill on the trip. Reminiscing, Pastor Teresa said, "From the minute we arrived in the airport, I could feel a heavy oppression in my spirit." She sensed the evil, and unfortunately her companion at the time did not join her in prayer. Unity in the face of evil is crucial.

We hadn't met Pastor Teresa at the time, but still I said playfully, "You should have traveled with us! We had an extraordinary airport experience!"

"Why didn't you take me with you?" she joked and prompted me to share our Chinese airport adventure.

Ed, Kevin, and I had traveled together. We entered the airport and approached immigration. I felt a vibration in my feet that became stronger by the moment. Having experienced airports that had collapsed in the past, I thought perhaps this airport was poorly constructed. We were close to the front doors of the terminal so it didn't seem possible, yet I wondered if it was the vibration of planes landing on the runway that I was feeling. At the same time, I suspected something different was happening, but dared not name it.

Ed has lots of aviation engineering experience, so I asked, "Can we feel the runway vibrations in here? My feet are vibrating."
"No," he answered, "but I feel something, too...."
"Me, too," Kevin said. "But I don't think it's the runway!" He started laughing in an unusual way that confirmed my suspicions.

The experience was too large, too awe-inspiring to speak about it. Finally, I got up courage and said, "It's the Holy Spirit." Kevin started laughing harder and nodding his head. We all started to laugh under the power of the Holy Spirit. The feeling increased and expanded rising higher and higher in our bodies to a shaking sensation. Though evil spirits tried to block our entry to the nation, the Holy Spirit turned it all to our advantage. He was saying in His own unique way, "Welcome to China!"

Bridge for Peace Foundation for Freedom

Our host met us and said he had received a phone call the night before tipping him off. The caller said Ed, Kevin, and I would be arrested when we entered the airport. This caused our host to take certain precautions which resulted in a great blessing as we interacted with government officials. Territorial spirits failed, God glorified His name.

Pastor Teresa, a woman of prayer and greatly used by the Holy Spirit, sensed the situation, but her traveling companion did not stand with her in prayer. There is danger when our companions cause discord.

10) Can you share an experience when you knew the Devil was stirred up against you but you had more awareness of God's power?

_____

_____

_____

_____

_____

11) How can you cultivate a greater awareness of God's presence when the Devil is making his oppressive power very apparent to you?

_____

_____

_____

_____

_____

_____

A Course in Deliverance

SNAKE- FREE ZONE

B4P takes authority over our territory by establishing a Snake-Free Zone. While on mission in North Carolina, USA, a team member sensed small snakes attempting to divide us. Small snakes of irritation, misinterpretation of a word spoken, and comparison try to disrupt mission teams. We formed a circle, arms behind each other's backs, and each one brought their heels together. Then we touched our toes to our teammates' toes all around the circle in a prophetic dramatization.

God called His prophets to "act out" His Word. (Ezekiel 4:1-13, Jeremiah 32:6) We declared through body language that we would not let little snakes come between us. We laughed as some of us overbalanced in an exaggeration of what ballet calls first position. Evil spirits hate when we laugh like kids. God told me holy laughter is like machine gun fire into hell. (Remember how we laughed entering China?)

Simplicity, humility, and the enjoyment of one another create an atmosphere the Devil hates. In the Snake-Free Zone we sometimes physically support each other so we all succeed in standing. Mutual support and team work is an abomination to the enemy.

In B4P we have a lot of fun, but we aren't joking around. We seriously attack the enemy with the charism of joy. The Snake-Free Zone is a powerful tool of deliverance. When the circle is formed and the group is ready, anyone being harassed can get into the middle.

When someone enters the circle's center, the group prays for them in the name of Jesus. This is not a childish exercise, but it is child-like. Jesus invited us to come to Him with the simple, trusting attitude of a child. The arrogant, prideful, or self-aggrandizing will struggle to enter the circle. Power is released in the Snake-Free Zone when we enter and pray as one.

We prayed this dramatization with Fr. Peter in Europe. He declared, "My room has been baptized in the Snake-Free Zone." Since then, many territories have been delivered through praying the B4P Snake-Free Zone.

12) Try out the Snake-Free Zone for yourself and bind territorial and harassing spirits. In your study group, circle up, heels together, touch toes with your neighbors on either side of you. Most likely you will need to support each other. You'll soon find out you have to get in close to make it work! If you don't have anyone to stand with you at the moment, stand up yourself and declare your own Snake-Free Zone. What did you experience? What did you observe?

_____

_____

_____

_____

_____

_____

Moses battled the prince of Egypt, a spirit using Pharaoh. Not a low ranking spirit, but a territorial spirit that had enslaved the Israelites. Moses carried a message through his devouring snake. God said to the territorial spirit in today's vernacular, "I'll eat you alive." Do not fear the demonic. Know spirits of darkness exist. Take your responsibility seriously. Overcome evil spirits by the power of God. Rejoice in Jesus Christ who set us free and empowered us to free others, giving glory to His name.

Chapter Five

Rule over Rebellion

The Israelite exit from Egypt was a miraculous and harrowing experience. God's glory towered over them as a flaming cloud, Egyptian soldiers pursued them from behind, and the Red Sea parted in front of them. Moses wiped his brow. At the same time he hoped to wipe away the memory of Pharaoh's arrogant face contorted with defiance. Moses heaved a sigh of relief. The power struggle was over, or so he thought. Unfortunately, he was premature. A new contender lurked in the shadows, rallying support. Unsuspecting Moses didn't hear the gossip, didn't notice the furtive glances, but he had an enemy in his camp. (Numbers 16:1–17:10)

Korah, a prominent figure among the Israelites, was discontented. A popular leader, he influenced men by complaining of hardship and condemning Moses's leadership. The men listened to Korah. Their discontent grew into envy and produced rebellion. Eventually, the malcontents stirred up the community against Moses and Aaron. Over 250 prominent men defied Moses and demanded more control. Their tribe was chosen to minister to God and His people, but they craved power like the pagan Egyptian sorcerers. The example of Egyptian priesthood contaminated them. Grasping at imagined political authority and the accompanying sumptuous lifestyle, they balked at a vocation of service to God and His people.

Moses was blindsided. He never expected the people he served to oppose him. Shocked, he lay face down on the ground before the Lord. Then he rose to deliver the Lord's message to the Israelites. God was about to make His choice plain. Moses threw the Israelite's accusations back in their faces, "You are the ones who have gone too far!"

Then Moses cooled down. He tried to reason with them. A good leader, he reminded them of their special role. He cautioned them, "You have been chosen from among all the people to minister in God's tabernacle and to minister to the people." He explained that God had honored them and they were revolting against the Lord. God assigned them their leadership positions and set limits on their authority.

Moses sent them a message of reconciliation and a request to meet. Moses showed forgiveness. He initiated the process of reconciliation. He was ready to work toward a resolution. In deliverance ministry, forgiveness is key. For an in-depth study and discussion on the importance of forgiveness see *Foundation for Healing*.

1) Moses models righteousness when confronted by the rebellious. What steps does Moses take to overcome the spirit of rebellion?

_____

_____

_____

_____

_____

REBELLION

The Israelites reject Moses's appeal and send an arrogant response. They accuse him, saying, "You took us from beautiful Egypt, a land of milk and honey! You led us into this wilderness! We'll die here! You treat us like your subjects. And besides, you haven't given us fields or vineyards. We refuse to meet with you!"

Moses's anger boils over. He complains to God, stating his innocence. Under God's authority, he challenges Korah to a showdown. "Turn up here tomorrow with your 250 followers. Aaron will be here with me."

The whole community sides with Korah. Every one of them betrays Moses. Fuming with anger, they turn up for the face-off. In a blaze, God's glory appears. The Lord cautions Moses and Aaron to move away. God intends to destroy all the rebels immediately.

Moses and Aaron fall on their faces and pray for the people's lives. Despite the abuse they have undergone, they plead for mercy for the Israelites. God responds. He commands Moses to tell the people to back away from the tents of the three ringleaders. Moses warned them, they were defying God. It was God's authority they had rejected. It was God they called a liar, complaining that He had not fulfilled His promises. They wanted everything He promised to them instantly, on their own terms. They accused the Lord, Who freed them from Egyptian slavery, of depriving them of their former fine land and lush life. They blamed God for their struggles, as God was leading them into the promise. Now, God will settle the question of authority. He tells Moses if the people want to be saved, they must not stand with the instigators.

Imagine the scene. Moses rushes to the tents of the ringleaders. "Quick, get away! Get away from these wicked men! You will know I have been sent by God and have obeyed His commands. I have done nothing on my own. All I have done the Lord has commanded me to do." Moses falls silent as a rumble in the air intensifies like thunder. The ground heaves. People scream. The earth cracks open. People wail as they plunge into the fissure. All those who stood with the wicked are swallowed up alive. Their coveted belongings plummet alongside them. The earth closes over them. They vanish. People bolt in all directions, terrified that the earth will consume them. Fire flashes out from the Lord and the 250 rebel leaders die instantly. A horrifying day.

Exhausted, the Israelites sleep fitfully that night. Finally, the sun's golden rays light the horizon. The Israelites face the new dawn in a foul mood. The whole community grumbles in one raucous voice. "Moses and Aaron, you have killed the Lord's people."

How had a second rebellion formed overnight? Men had died, but the demonic spirit of rebellion had not died with them. The people who were spared had not repented. They continued to grumble. Their complaining opened the door to demonic influence in their souls. Immediately, a plague of retribution spreads among them killing thousands. Moses and Aaron act swiftly. Aaron fills the incense burner, lights it, and stands between the dead and the living making atonement for them. Aaron's act of penitence frees them from the consequences of their sin. The plague stops. (Numbers 16:41-50)

BEARING FRUIT

The Lord resolves to end the complaints against Moses and Aaron. When chaos reigns, failure follows. Moses's mission must succeed. Order must be restored. God will settle the question of authority. He issues instructions to Moses: "Each tribal leader, as well as Aaron, must carve his name on his wooden staff. These staffs will be given to you. You will put them in the Tabernacle. Rest them in front of the Ark of the Covenant where I meet with you. Buds will sprout on the staff belonging to the leader I choose. I will put an end to this murmuring and complaining against you."

They did what the Lord commanded. Night falls. While people sleep the staffs rest in God's presence. Twelve sticks of dead wood lie before the Ark of the Covenant, a sacred chest overlaid with pure gold inside and outside. The cover is solid gold. Two cherubim formed of hammered gold are attached to it. They face each other looking down on the cover, their wings spread wide. This is where God meets and speaks with Moses. Now, unbroken silence reigns, deep and still.

God's glory emanates from the Ark of the Covenant, hidden from human eyes. God chooses. Sap runs swiftly through a dry staff. The gentle sound glides through the silence like a flowing creek. Green shoots crackle as they press through the wood. Almond buds form and unfold to delight their God. Tender pink petals perfume the tabernacle with penetrating sweetness. Fuzzy almond fruits take shape. Their green flesh supernaturally matures while hidden in the holy place. The fruit is warm as if the sun had ripened it. The skins burst displaying the almonds within.

Dawn breaks, rays of sun shoot across the cloudless blue sky. Moses enters the tabernacle and collects the evidence. The people wait for the verdict. Whose wooden staff will show the miraculous sign of sprouting? Moses reappears, raises Aaron's staff, and stirs the air with it. Aaron's staff budded, blossomed, and produced almonds. People are happy with mere buds, but God desires fruit.

People are happy with mere buds, but God desires fruit.

God chose to give Moses and Aaron His authority. They were to use their authority to lead the people into the Promised Land. God says He has chosen us. Don't be satisfied with buds. Stay in His presence and you will flower giving off the fragrance of life. You will bear fruit to glorify God. His authority will be seen in you.

2) Jesus tell us what God has done for us, what He requires from us, and what He will do for us in the future. What does Jesus say in John 15:16? What is fruit that will last?

_____

_____

_____

_____

_____

_____

God's heart is in us, because when we pray for deliverance we want to see fruit that lasts, too. My courageous friend told me of a spiritual battle she has engaged in on behalf of a boy. "I've seen some change, but I'm wondering what I'm missing. I'm not having the victory in this. What do you think?"

"I think the problem is right there," I answered. "Satan has made you believe you are not having victory. Christ has the victory. So you have it, too."

A Course in Deliverance

Satan is watching your progress. Scripture tells us Satan stopped tempting Jesus for the moment. Satan would wait for a better time. (Luke 4:13) He pays attention to timing. He deploys tricky demons to derail us at the crucial moment. Scripture tells us when to expect the attack. Song of Solomon 2:15 cautions us to capture these sly little foxes that damage our vineyards, the place where the Holy Spirit is growing us up to produce fruit. Notice when those sharp-clawed, pointy-toothed foxes tear up the field. The rampage begins when the vineyard is in bloom. Satan will intensify the attack when you are aromatic with the fragrance of life. When the promises of God ripen and you are about to bear fruit Satan will send out his minions to disrupt the process. Satan does not want you to bear godly fruit. His pet foxes of doubt and fear can cause severe blossom rot!

3) What can help you expel "little foxes" from areas where you may be vulnerable? (Read Song of Solomon 2:15.)

_____

_____

_____

_____

_____

_____

PERSEVERANCE

The Holy Spirit taught me this principle of perseverance through experience. I became friends with Jackie, a powerful intercessor. She was tormented by a demon. At night it attacked her. I wanted to pray for Jackie when the demon tormented her. Finally, I had the opportunity. Karen and I overnighted with her. In the middle of the night, she said, "It's here." Her jaw started grinding as the spirit brutally twisted her face. We prayed the blood of Jesus, the blood of Jesus. She called out in pain and suffered greatly. Finally, it left her.

I asked the Lord, "What am I missing?" God said, "Nothing." We have to persevere. Satan wants you to believe you are inadequate, to question yourself, to doubt that you are gifted in deliverance. It is all a lie. Christ is more than adequate in us, He is the answer. Believe in His Word that says you will drive out demons. (Mark 16:17)

God brought a dead staff to life as it lay before the Ark of the Covenant and caused it to produce fruit. We can learn a lot from resurrected dead wood! If God can cause that staff to bear fruit, what are you worried about? Rest in God's presence, stand on Christ's defeat of Satan through His blood, and you will produce fruit. God chose you to accomplish what He wants.

4) God counsels us about abiding. He tells us that to bear fruit, we must abide in Him. What does this mean to you? Share an experience of abiding in Him.

_____

_____

_____

_____

_____

_____

BREAKING CURSES

Everyone was baffled. Cynthia, a faithful woman in her forties, a caring professional, and an inspiration to friends and family, had received prayer many times without any relief. "I don't know why she hasn't been healed. It's so terrible. I've invited her to the B4P ministry this Thursday," her friend told me.

Thursday rolled around and I entitled my message, "What is this Fire!?" I encouraged people to receive the power of God. His consuming fire was present to burn up every spiritual enemy of our souls. A holy blaze burned in our hearts that night to see every captive set free. When prayer time came I asked to minister to Cynthia. After speaking God's Word, B4P invites those with the most pain to come first to be relieved.

Broad smile on her pretty face, Cynthia hobbled forward. I found it very painful to watch her. She suffered with swollen knuckles and lame feet filled with inflammation, fluid, and nagging arthritic pain. Having been miraculously healed from arthritis myself, I felt great empathy. She told me many people had prayed for her. Many had said she would be healed. She believed in God's miracle-working power. She knew Jesus had shed His blood for her healing. She was active in her church and had already been baptized in the Holy Spirit. I asked if she

A Course in Deliverance

needed to forgive anyone. She thought for a moment and then said there was no one she hadn't forgiven. I said, "Let's pray, believing together for your healing."

After asking permission, I placed my hand on her shoulder and prayed healing scriptures. Gently, I held her other hand watching for a change. Cynthia agreed as I prayed, saying, "Yes, yes. Thank you, Jesus." We continued to pray together, thanking Jesus and releasing healing. I periodically checked in with Cynthia, asking her how she was doing and if anything was different. "We are looking for any change at all, even a small change."

"My stomach feels like it is churning," she responded. Stomach distress during prayer can indicate demonic activity. Because Cynthia shared this, I changed tactics.

I said, "In the name of Jesus, spirit of infirmity you must go." Cynthia said, "No." Surprised, I looked into her face. She shook her head and said again," No."
Then I realized she was not speaking, but the demonic spirit was speaking through her. I said, "You must go, now."

Believe in His Word that says you will drive out demons.

The demonic spirit gave a snide answer. "Oh, really." It wasn't a question, it was a statement. It wasn't planning to budge, but this was not a contest of wills. It was a matter of Cynthia's legal spiritual inheritance through Jesus Christ. I continually and calmly repeated the truth. "In the name of Jesus, by His authority through His blood, you must go."

After some time she said, "I see a door." I got excited. A door is a good symbol to me. Then Cynthia said, "It's a prison door." I heard dread in her voice. *What*? Again I was surprised, but revelation came. I knew God had bound rebellious angels. (Jude 1:6) And the demons had asked Jesus not to order them into the Abyss, the deep bottomless pit where dark spirits are detained. (Luke 8:31) And so I said, "In the name of Jesus, I command you to go back to the place you came from." She told me her churning stomach had settled. I knew that was a sign of victory.

I had my hand beneath hers and I saw her swollen knuckles shrink. I asked her, "How are your hands?" She looked them over carefully and said, "The same." "Okay," I said. I was only mildly surprised at this. Sometimes people cannot see the change I see. I could be seeing by faith what will be or Satan may blind the prayer recipient to change. Either way, seeing change was important to Cynthia's healing.

Ed became free and I asked him to join us for a bit. I had been praying with Cynthia for over an hour. Ed sat with us, repeating truth. I was renewed after a few minutes of Ed's support and he went back to his ministry team. I continued to pray. Finally she said, "It's gone." We thanked and praised Jesus.

Then Cynthia said, "I see a cauldron in my head." A cauldron is a place where witches brew and store spells and curses. It is a symbol of witchcraft. I asked about forgiveness again, as the Holy Spirit may have shown her something new. Her heart was free of resentment and unforgiveness. In the name of Jesus I broke every curse that had been spoken over her. In the authority of Jesus's name, as His servant, I canceled every curse that had come down through the generations. Healing and deliverance belonged to her because of her inheritance in Christ.

She said, "I see many papers over my head. They are assignments." I understood her spiritual vision was clearing. She saw the orders the enemy had given to demonic powers, and recognized them for what they were. Cynthia held a public position with authority over many people. Perhaps a disgruntled person toying with witchcraft had cursed her. She may have unknowingly married into a curse against women in her spouse's family line. A curse may have been in her family tree. I did not know the specifics, but I put every assignment of the enemy through the blood of Jesus and declared them void. These assignments kept her from seeing the improvement in her hands. Whatever other purpose they served, they were meant to discourage her.

Cynthia noticed the swelling in her fingers had gone down. The assignment against Cynthia that had blinded her to improvements was broken! Her ankles showed creases that weren't there before because the swelling reduced. She felt better physically and she felt relieved within herself.

5) What did you notice about this encounter? Did you find something helpful?

_____

_____

_____

_____

Usually, when praying with someone for healing, I encourage the person I am praying for not to pray but to receive. This is very important in healing prayer. As I pray for them I watch and wait to see what will unfold. In Cynthia's case, I sensed from the beginning she needed to participate with me in stating truth. Indeed, she needed to take a warrior's stance and refuse to allow the demon to harass her.

Chapter 5
Rule Over Rebellion

A Course in Deliverance

6) Receiving is crucial in healing prayer as explained in *Foundation for Healing*. Insisting on our own freedom is essential in deliverance. Comment on these two statements.

_____

_____

_____

_____

_____

_____

_____

HOLY DEMAND

My job was to pray scriptural truth and enforce the finished work of the cross on this demon. This is why we must know our *Foundation for Freedom*.

Notice demonic activity was progressively exposed. The first clue was a "churning stomach." Queasiness, nausea, even vomiting can accompany demonic activity. When Cynthia said her stomach was "churning" I understood that our prayers disturbed the demonic spirit's comfort. It began to stir. It was being ousted by the blood of Jesus and began to respond.

The demonic spirit shamelessly used Cynthia's mouth in open rebellion when I told it to go. We identified rebellious spirits in Pharaoh and Korah. Cynthia was not a rebellious person. However, the demonic spirit that inhabited her had stolen her inheritance of health, inflicted pain, and showed direct rebellion against God. This spirit refused to submit. Demons want to remain in the body they inhabit at all costs.

The spirit of darkness then challenged my authority. When I said, "You must go," the demon responded, "Oh, really." I felt insulted at first. The nerve of that demon! After my reaction I laughed to myself, because I know the common strategies of demons. Satan tries to get our egos involved. He will always ask, "Who do you think you are?"

Moses told Pharaoh, "This is what the Lord God says… 'Let my people go.'" Pharaoh retorted, "Is that so? And who is the Lord that I should listen to Him and let Israel go?" (Exodus 5:1-2) The same rebellious spirit that spoke through Pharaoh speaks today. Demons mocked our

Master on the cross and they continue to use mockery as a weapon to demoralize us. I was not entering into a power struggle with the Devil.

Do you recall when God said the Israelites were rebelling against Him, not Moses? As Moses thought they were challenging him, we can easily think the challenge is between the demonic spirits and us. They will try to get you to fight on that ground. Don't fall for it.

The rebels wanted to take charge, to usurp Moses's God-given position. Demons still have the same objective. We have authority in Christ. If our pride gets involved and we exert human authority to battle the Devil out of our egos we no longer function as ambassadors of Christ. We become rebels if we put ourselves in God's place. And we will always lose to the Devil. I have seen colossal battles when people use the name of Jesus, but they are not submitted to His authority. They scream and carry on trying to deliver someone. The demonized person suffers. And the whole encounter is a joke to the demon. I have seen deliverance ministry riddled with pride as it becomes an issue of power. Be clear, Jesus is the one with the power. We are His chosen instruments. His power operates through us.

Thousands of years later, this demon in Cynthia was using the same old pattern, because he has found it to be continually successful. The demon meant to put me off balance. I know Jesus destroyed the work of the enemy at His cross. God has full authority. By God's grace, I saw the trap.

Remember, the demonic challenged Jesus. Through a human pawn a demon demanded of Jesus, "Tell us by what authority you are doing these things?" (Luke 20:2) Jesus stood His ground and threw the opposition into confusion. They found no way out and left. They waited for a more favorable time to challenge Him again. As Luke 20:20 says, "Watching for their opportunity, the leaders sent secret agents pretending to be honest men. They tried to get Jesus to say something that could be reported. . . ."

7) Undoubtedly, you will meet this same spirit that will challenge God's authority in you. You may have met it already. It still sounds the same after thousands of years. What do you do in the name of Jesus that Satan objects to? Fill in the blank. "By what authority do you_____. Now fill in your name. I,_____, have been authorized by Jesus Christ, Savior of the world, Creator of everything that has been created.

There is an emotion called righteous anger. When I see demonic spirits harassing and even tormenting people, I often feel righteous anger. This is different from the anger that comes from injured pride. Righteous anger is God's heart motivating our own.

8) Comment on your experience with righteous anger, drawing on Scripture or personal experience.

A Course in Deliverance

_____

_____

_____

_____

_____

_____

_____

When Cynthia shared her vision of a door, I thought the Holy Spirit was showing Cynthia a new future and I rejoiced. Jesus says knock and the door will be opened. (Matthew 7:7) God says He will give the despairing a door of hope. (Hosea 2:15) Paul talks about a great door for effective work opened to him though he faced opposition. (1Corinthians 16:9) God says He places an open door before us that no one can shut. (Revelation 3:20) Hope, productive work in times of struggle, and a door God opens that cannot be closed! These are good signs. When Cynthia unexpectedly revealed, "It's a prison door," I was again surprised.

The vision shook her. She felt imprisoned by arthritis. I thank the Holy Spirit who immediately spoke to me. This demonic spirit was not free to inflict a child of God. The Holy Spirit reminded me it had been disarmed, made powerless by Jesus. "Send the demon back to prison." (Colossians 2:15)

I rebuked the demon. I said, "In the name of Jesus Christ, go back to the place you came from." Her stomach settled. A good sign, but we weren't finished yet.

DELIVERED FROM WITCHCRAFT

Pharaoh rebelled against God's message. Korah rebelled against Moses. The Korah rebellion ended, but the Israelites continued to rebel against God. In the Bible, rebellion is likened to the sin of witchcraft. (1Samuel 15:23) Cynthia never participated in witchcraft, but clearly the spirit of witchcraft was involved in afflicting her.

Spirits of witchcraft drive manipulation, intimidation, and domination. When one person tries to control another the spirit of witchcraft is involved. This spirit does not only use spells and incantations, it uses methods that are "socially acceptable" in some circles. This includes sarcasm, passive aggressive behavior, and mockery. Some people use anger to control others. When we understand the spiritual implication of behaviors it can change our response. I knew a very controlling person. When I understood a spirit of darkness was trying to get at me through them, I changed my response and our relationship shifted for the better.

Dissension is healthy. I appreciate people who thoughtfully challenge concepts, bring a different viewpoint to the table, and cautiously guard us from pitfalls. This is different from the person who argues everything, resists every suggestion, and throws up roadblocks to progress as demonstrated by Korah.

Every one of us is capable of rebellion. Hebrews 3:8 cautions us not to harden our hearts as the Israelite rebels did while following Moses through the desert. We must pay attention to our heart's condition. Moses was angry with his accusers, but he prayed for God to show them mercy. He turned away from vengeance.

God knows us so well. The Bible's accuracy amazes me. At times, I have felt a physical hardness in my heart. At those times I have to deliver myself from whatever attitude has caused hardness by dealing with the person or situation God's way. We have to be alert to unforgiveness or bitterness in our hearts. As Moses said to Korah, we are not rebelling against people, but rebelling against God.

I remember a black and white boxing movie we watched on television as kids. The trainer reminded the boxer of the one-two punch. It was two fast blows, one with the left, and one with the right. The point was to deliver a knock-out to the opponent. One day God told me, "Remember the POW in My power. The Devil is KO'd." The one-two punch we deliver to the Devil is 1) by forgiveness and 2) by prayer.

God says forgive and pray for our enemies. Jesus wants us to live in the joy of freedom! (Ezekiel 36:26) God says He will take away our stony hearts and give us a heart of obedience to Him. We are delivered through repentance and prayer.

God sometimes asks me to pray for particular people as a long term assignment. He mentioned a name to me of a public figure and I found my heart had a stone in it. I had hardness in my heart toward him. Have you ever resented anyone? Then you can understand what I mean. I knew that was wrong, so I truly repented. Now the acid test was praying for the man. I did not instantaneously feel different, but I wanted to obey God. I found a picture of this public figure as a small boy on his tricycle and put it in my Bible. Over a period of time, my attitude has changed. Because of God, I am sure my prayers have benefited the man, but I too have received a benefit. I have been delivered! I no longer have hardness in my heart, but the love of God has moved in and taken over.

9) Galatians 3:1 (Amplified Bible) begins, "O you poor and silly and thoughtless and unreflecting and senseless Galatians. Who has fascinated or bewitched or cast a spell over you...." The passage reminds us it is possible to be enticed through an ungodly fascination. What is our safeguard? (Read Galatians 3:1-7)

_____

_____

_____

_____

_____

Chapter Six

The Piercing Sword

It was a bitter cold day in December and Christmas wasn't far off. Ed and I serve a ministry that distributes food while preaching the Gospel. At Christmas we supply truckloads of gifts to families unable to purchase them. Families come to a local school. Children come with them, because most don't have babysitters. They enter to live worship music and move on to the gym where cardboard cartons hold teddy bears and baby dolls. Board games, puzzles, and even bicycles wait to be claimed. Toting bags of toys, they turn the corner into a hallway where Ed and I wait. We offer free Bibles and pamphlets. We pray for everyone who would like prayer. Ed and I watched for the next bunch of people when a youngster appeared. He was a little over three feet tall. He had found a plastic sword, almost as big as he was, and claimed it as his own. It was unboxed!

The sword probably came from a Full Armor of God playset. The red and gray plastic helmet, shield, and sword were inspired by Ephesians 6:10 that counsels us to put on the whole armor of God. The Bible says fasten on God's armor to stand against the Devil's schemes.

The armor includes the belt of truth we fasten around our waists. The breastplate of righteousness covers our hearts. The gospel of peace readies our feet. The shield of faith guards us. The helmet of salvation protects our minds. Finally, we clutch the sword of the Spirit which is the word of God.

Now this little guy in the hallway was swinging the plastic sword of the Spirit like a wild man. *Swish, swish,* he sliced the air making a whistling sound with each swipe. He wielded that sword like he was fighting for his life. All of us stood back, from guys six foot tall to tots in the hallway. His mother yelled at him to stop, but she was not in his imaginary world and he ignored her.

I learned something important that afternoon. It doesn't matter how small or insignificant we are if we brandish the sword of the Spirit. Everyone backed up when this little guy lunged. Satan does the same when we attack with the sword of the Spirit. The Word of God causes Satan to back off, not the person who speaks it.

Bridge for Peace Foundation for Freedom

1) Read Ephesians 6:10-18. Make note of each piece of armor and its purpose.

_____

_____

_____

_____

_____

_____

Some Christians shudder at the thought of demons, tremble at the word deliverance, and shrink from the battle against witchcraft in its many forms. The occult looms, magnified by mystery like a menacing shadow purposefully exaggerated on the wall, threatening those who dare to look. God's power is just the opposite. His power brings joy like the rays of the sun and roaring waterfalls. His might is a comfort available to all, yet a hidden mystery. God invites us into His secret places to unveil his strength and empower us. A child of God can pick up His Word and expel a legion of sullen demons with the sword of the Spirit.

2) The sword of the Spirit is the Word of God. What does that mean to you? (Read Ephesian 6:10-18.)

_____

_____

_____

_____

_____

_____

_____

A Course in Deliverance

3) What does Hebrews 4:12 say about God's Word?

_____

_____

_____

_____

_____

_____

_____

GOD'S WORD FULL OF LIVING POWER

Though the Word of God is ancient it is alive and it is at work. God's Word produces results today in surprising ways. Nations rely on armaments. The world almanac reports the military strength of every nation on earth. However, the power in the Word of God can never be measured. No one has the ability to assess it. Some may question particular scriptures' relevance to daily living. God is not troubled by that, He just keeps fulfilling His Word, sometimes in unusual ways.

Ed and I joined Fr. Victor Darlington in Rome in 1998 as planned. God had brought the three of us together in New York. Fr. Victor often stayed in our home. We customarily include guests in our family prayer. As a result of our prayer with Fr. Victor, God called the three of us to begin the B4P Prayer Walk in Rome mission. While on mission, B4P has a team of intercessors. They are excellent prayer warriors, swift with the sword of the Spirit. They pray for the mission team and their families, and the mission activities. I am sure the intercessor team played a role in what occurred.

During the mission Fr. Victor received a message from his mother in Nigeria. He was bursting to tell us what had happened.

Mrs. Darlington was a stately and elderly woman. She always hired the same driver to take her into town when she had a need. On this occasion, she and her driver sped down the familiar road. An SUV roared up from behind, pulled alongside them, and forced them into a ditch. Four aggressors leaped from the vehicle and rushed his mother's hired car. As the bullies reached for the handles on the car doors, swarms of bees appeared and began to sting them! The men swatted wildly, while shouting with fear and pain as they were stung. They ran for the safety of their SUV. Mrs. Darlington's driver spun out, dirt spraying the would-be robbers' vehicle. Her driver cleared the ditch and their sedan raced down the road, proving God's promise in Exodus 23:28 applies to us today! He said He would send hornets to deliver us! God also says in this scripture He would help us defeat the people now living in the land. The terrible crime of car-jacking is on the rise, but God has His way of frustrating the enemies' plans.

4) Can you give an example of God's Word bringing deliverance in your life?

_____

_____

_____

_____

_____

_____

That word about God sending hornets was written thousands of years ago. Certainly it was fulfilled before, but God released the power of the word again when the need arose.

CUT THROUGH DECEPTION

Ed and I stayed at a Christian retreat house situated on a farm in Massachusetts. The acreage sloped into a valley where hearty pumpkins grew. Green hills rose in the distance. A fellow guest advised us to take a trip to a nearby retreat house. Pointing to the hills outside of the window she said, "You shouldn't miss it. I've never felt such peace." Ed and I wanted to visit this new place to worship Jesus Christ the Prince of Peace and meet faithful people that we hadn't yet encountered. Checking our directions to the center, we took a drive passing maple trees and oaks in fall colors as we wound through the country road. Finding the place tucked away in the hills, we pulled into the parking lot and walked past the "Retreat Center" sign. Entering the dimly lit building, a weighty peace descended on us. It was remarkable. The guest master greeted us and was very welcoming. He explained their philosophy of meditative practices. it was then we learned that people worshipped falsed gods at this center. Surprised by that news, we hastened out of the place. As we walked back to our car I was puzzled by the brief experience. Though they worshipped many gods, the sense of peace was undeniable. I said to Ed, "Strange. The peace in there was so thick you could cut it with a knife." Immediately God said to me, "Yes. You can cut right through the veil of deception with the sword of truth."

A peaceful atmosphere can be created with the right music and insistence on hushed voices. That is a conditional, temporary state. Christ's peace is not dependent on externals. Christ purchased peace for us through the blood of His cross. When Christ lives within us, He changes us. We come to know His peace in every circumstance. Peace flows from our hearts into our world.

5) Jesus Christ gave us peace. Not the conditional peace of the world based on circumstances, but true supernatural peace that satisfies. (Read John 14:27.) What particular scripture acts as your sword of the Spirit when you need to touch God's peace?

_____

_____

_____

_____

_____

_____

I grew up with three siblings and Grandma lived with us. I remember my patient mother getting exasperated on occasion. She would say, "All I want is a little peace." Most people want peace. There are times in history when people wanted peace at any price. The Bible records lying prophets announcing, "Peace, peace." People believed the liars, even though God said war was coming. (Jeremiah 6:14)

A true formula for peace is:

- Ask ourselves if we have obeyed God.
- Repent if necessary. If we have been faithful, thank the Holy Spirit.
- Be reconciled to God.

Bridge for Peace Foundation for Freedom

Disregarding God's counsel, most of us don't even hope for peace. We just want to be numb, not to feel stressed, hurting, or alone. We deaden our soul with whatever works for us, from mindless movies to drugs.

God says superficial treatments are offered while people's wounds are killing them. The application of the blood of Jesus for deliverance is what people are dying for. A Muslim convert recalled the moment when Jesus Christ appeared to him. He raised his hands to the Lord and said, "My Lord, I'll die for You." Jesus answered him and said, "Don't do that. I've already done that. Live for Me."

Jesus wants us fully alive. Pick up the sword of the Spirit to set the captive free. A woman said to me, "Annette, please don't ever stop. There are so many of us desperate to be delivered. We'll go through whatever we have to for freedom."

People like surface treatments because they don't hurt, but if the need is deep they don't help either. Cutting out poison causes pain, but creates conditions for healing. The Word cuts out festering lies of the Devil that destroy lives. Lies only have power when someone believes them. Truth is truth whether or not we believe it. The sword of the Spirit, the Word of God, brings real deliverance. Christ delivers us and infuses our souls with peace through His power.

Deliverance does not have to be painful! Many times it is a swift and stunning testimony to God's power. Expect the manifestation of instantaneous deliverance, but be prepared to persevere if necessary.

6) What does the Word say about how Satan works? How does Scripture say Christ will destroy lies? (Read 2Thessalonians 2:8-11)

_____

_____

_____

_____

_____

_____

A Course in Deliverance

Ed and I arrived early for ministry at a familiar NY location. A woman from the music ministry told me, "Annette, we really need prayers. Seven people died from overdoses this week." I was stunned. "And they were all under 40 years old. What happens is they go into rehab and when they come out they go back to the high doses of drugs they took before, but their bodies can't handle it."

A man said, "Annette, please pray for my family. My nephew had taken painkillers for his back for some time now. He just overdosed and died. We don't think he meant to do it."

That night when I spoke to all the faithful people gathered, righteous anger burned in me. Ephesians 6 was on my mind. Take the sword of the Spirit which is the Word of God. God showed me an image. We have the sword of the Spirit in our hand and it is pointed outward. We stand our ground with the sword of the Spirit out in front, but rather than lunge at Satan we wait for our enemy to run into our sword and skewer himself.

When we do attack the Devil, sometimes our brothers object. I heard a preacher speak from the pulpit. He said, "I was in the subway yesterday. A person stood in the train preaching about God. Religion is a private matter. He should have been quiet." Later, I was at a backyard party. A church-going lady had been to the Coney Island boardwalk. She said, "A person stood on the boardwalk preaching Jesus. There are plenty of ways to find out about Jesus if people want to know. He should not be doing that."

People's spirits hear when the Word of God is spoken. The Word of God is the sword of the Spirit, stirring up demonic opposition. The Devil is brash. He's loud and he's bold. The enemy of our souls wants us to back up and get out of his way. The sword of the Spirit silences the Devil. When we speak the Word of God, bonds are severed. Captives go free. God calls us to speak the Word and clear out the demons.

7) Where do you see a need for the sword of the Spirit to bring truth? Compose a prayer to address the need. Include a verse of Scripture if possible, because the sword of the Spirit is the Word of God.

_____

_____

_____

_____

_____

_____

Bridge for Peace Foundation for Freedom

Jack is a man from a Christian teaching group that conducts conferences. During the conference, Jack brings plastic "armor of God gear" to the event. He asks a volunteer to put on the plastic imitations of the armor named in Ephesians—helmet, shield, sword, etc. Jack then organizes a dramatization of the spiritual battle between a Christian and a demon. He told me, "We've had conferences all over the nation with all kinds of Christian groups. When we get to this demonstration, it is always the same. The Christian uses the shield against the 'demon' to fend off attacks, but never the sword." To interpret his experience, we are in a defensive mode protecting what we have, but not demanding the release of stolen territory.

On mission in China for the first time, our hosts took us to a festival in a massive park. Seated on the grass, we watched the programs on stage. Our host urged us, "Go on up. They want volunteers!" Ed declined, but Kevin and I jogged over. People enjoyed our antics, and Kevin was asked to stay on. They dressed him in a white samurai costume. His opponent was in black. The "contest" was on national television news. The symbolism was plain. A battle was raging in China. Kevin liberally used his sword and though he had no previous samurai training, he won.

We need to be shaken out of our lethargy and enter the fight.

We are assured that we have spiritual weapons to demolish demonic strongholds, every pretension that sets itself up against the knowledge of God. (2 Corinthians 10:4-5) We need to be shaken out of our lethargy and enter the fight. I am sure there is a demonic spirit named lethargy. Many of us need to be set free from it.

A Filipino man asked me for prayer. He said, "I used to do what you do." He had been very active in evangelism in the Philippines. He regularly traveled into cities and rural areas, and many people were healed when he prayed for them in the name of Jesus. He accompanied the clergy on many healing missions. When he immigrated to Australia he had "been bullied at work." Eventually, he had a nervous breakdown. "I am now on disability. Can you pray for me?"

"Satan is a bully," I explained. "Demonic spirits want to inhabit a human body to inflict suffering. They want to control the one they enter. They also want to use that person to harm others. The person who bullied you allowed themselves to be used. Satan is a robber. He has been robbing you of your inheritance. He wants to keep you from serving God in the gifts of healing Christ has given you. Satan is also robbing the body of Christ, because we are not benefiting from what God put in you. And God is being robbed of glory that He deserves." I asked him if he could forgive the person who had harmed him. He said, "I've already done that."

I prayed for his deliverance and restoration. I advised him, "Brother, the best thing you can do now is to begin to pray for people."

He laughed. "When I'm healed I will."

A Course in Deliverance

"Brother, Jesus Christ has given you His healing. You know that. As you step out in faith and serve Him by praying for others, you will see your healing manifest."

"As soon as I'm better, I'll do that."

I always hope, but he appeared more convinced of his inability than his ability in Christ or Christ's ability in him. The Word of God tells us to resist the Devil and he will flee, but some Christians seem more resistant to what the Word of God says. Invested in postponing his restoration, he played into the enemy's hand. He knew about the sword of the Spirit, but it dangled limply at his side. Remember the example of Cynthia in Chapter 5, and the assignments against her? I mentioned that she had to enter the spiritual battle with me. She rebuked Satan, she resisted him. Unlike this gentleman, Cynthia had her sword drawn, sharpened, and piercing the target.

At a home meeting, Josephine mentioned, "That person made me furious. I won't forgive them." I knew I needed to talk with Josephine. A serious Christian, she told me she had sought counseling from the church. A wonderful woman, well known in the church community, had counseled with Josephine. Josephine was told God was patient and in time she would learn to forgive. Josephine said, "I'm waiting to be ready to forgive. God says I don't have to forgive yet. I'm waiting to be healed first and then I'll forgive." Lethargy was encouraged. In other words, wait around until enough time passes and you feel ready. Tomorrow is not guaranteed to anyone. I didn't want to contradict, but I had to speak truth. Jesus said forgive now. (Luke 6:37, 11:4, 17:4, 23:34)

Forgiveness is a decision we make. Then God brings healing to transform the feeling. If we wait until we "feel" like forgiving, Satan will capitalize on that. If we obey, God will bring the needed healing.

Josephine made the decision to forgive with many tears. Then she said, "Oh. Oh, I feel so good." Crying again she said, "I felt at night I was going mad because of the unforgiveness. I'm sure I got diabetes from it...." Unforgiveness caused other problems in her life. Where does God say we don't have to forgive until we feel up to it? Friends, most examples of demonization I am using in this book are from faithful people who love God, attend church, and seek counsel when they suspect they are out of their depth. Let us commit to studying God's Word and giving God's solutions to gripping problems.

Too few of us recognize when we are being manipulated by the Devil. The Devil is not everywhere, but there is more demonic activity in this world than most suspect. Don't focus on the Devil. I encourage you again, when you detect demonic involvement, be more aware of God's power for deliverance than of the Devil's presence.

Bridge for Peace Foundation for Freedom

In Revelation, Jesus is pictured with a sharp double-edged sword coming out of His *mouth*. A fearsome image! If there is an image opposite of lethargy, that has got to be it. Deception will fall, lies will be obliterated, and Satan will have nothing left. We can't fight against principalities and powers with carnal weapons. Let the sword of the Spirit come out of your mouth from this day forward. Are you the champion God created you to be? Set captives free with His Word now.

God wants to make you His mouthpiece but there are conditions.

Jeremiah 15:19 tells us to distinguish between the precious and the vile and we will be as God's own mouth! God says He wants you to be His mouthpiece! God says if you utter worthy and not worthless words, you will be His spokesman.

8) God wants to make you His mouthpiece, but there are conditions. Do you allow the Spirit to fill your heart and mouth with worthy and precious words? Comment on the scripture. (Read Jeremiah 15:19)

_____

_____

_____

_____

_____

_____

_____

In Tanzania I was able to use the few Swahili words I know. Oddly enough, among them was the word *now*. *Sasa* is the Swahili translation. Many people we prayed for said they would see how they felt the next day. Or they knew God would heal them someday. All sorts of postponements proliferated. The attitude of postponement is a trick. At the rally I burst out, "Sasa, sasa, sasa. We serve a sasa God, a *now* God!" And indeed, people started to receive healings immediately when Satan's trick that keeps us in bondage was exposed.

Waiting for healing and deliverance can look virtuous, patient and holy. But it is just a trick like the other vile tricks Satan plays. He deceives people by convincing them that true holiness requires patience. He tells us we should silently wait for relief in the distant future. He does this because he wants to occupy our territory. He wants us to tolerate his presence. People who need deliverance are rarely willing to postpone freedom. They are hurting, desperate,

A Course in Deliverance

and want to be freed by our *now* God. However, if they are duped into believing God wants them to wait around to be set free, these souls will patiently fold their hands, clench their teeth, and bear with the Devil.

9) What does God say about His willingness to help? When is God willing to help? (Read 2Corinthians 6:1-2)

_____

_____

_____

_____

_____

_____

_____

SMOKE AND MIRRORS

Many people spend their nights in torment. Unholy dreams and visitations haunt them. Ed and I ministered to Shirley who suffered for years from torturous dreams. She said, "I'm afraid to sleep. This has been happening as long as I remember." Evil spirits terrorized her. She felt their brutality in her physical body. She loved Jesus and was used mightily by God. She was baptized in the Spirit and active in church. Still, the demonic spirits harassed her. Friend, plenty of people who love Jesus and regularly attend church need help. If you are among them, there is no shame in that. Jesus shed His blood for us because He knew we needed it.

I have a lot of dream experience. God often tells me what to do in dreams. He warns me of dangers and how to respond. He explains Scripture to me in dreams, and shows me prophetic dreams that later occur in the world. God taught me spiritual warfare over a course of months through dreams. All of my prior "visitation" dreams have brought angelic spirits as messengers and instructors.

Ed and I prayed for Shirley in the name of Jesus for several days. She had some improvement. After about a week of ministering to her, I had a gruesome dream. When I awoke after the grisly dream, I still felt it. Mourning the loss in the dream situation weighed heavily on me. It was so real.

This dream was "real" in that it was more than a dream. I know the difference. Evil spirits sent me a threatening message. This never happened to me before or since, but it opened a way for the Holy Spirit to teach me. Later that same morning of the dream, we were traveling with Shirley. I told her, "I can really empathize with you now. It feels real. It still feels real. Certainly, it was more than a dream. But it *isn't* real."

The Word does not deny that terrors will try to bring fear; but the Word says by the power of God they will not succeed.

The Holy Spirit stirred like a favorable wind. Jesus Christ the Bright Morning Star pierced the dark cloud in my understanding. I navigated by the light He gave me. Slowly, I spoke out loud as I began to see. "The mental memory is alive and seems so real. The body response feels real, but it's a lie! It feels like it happened, but it didn't happen!" Obviously, I had not been physically harmed. "It is deception, smoke and mirrors! If we talk about it like it is real, we give Satan power. It was a deceiving dream." Shirley got it! God's anointing fell on us. I couldn't stop making up songs of praise and singing them very loudly! I was driving at the time and bouncing in my seat. The car was rocking as we praised God. All of heaven celebrated with us. I felt them singing, "They've got it! They've got it!"

It is time to take the sword of the Spirit and deflate fear. It is time to bring God's light into the shadow where the enemy lurks. The sword of the Spirit I pulled out of the Word for Shirley and me in that moment was Psalm 91, verse 5a. "You will not fear the terrors of the night." The Word does not deny that terrors will try to bring fear; but the Word says by the power of God they will not succeed.

10) Can you name a fear that has been in the shadows in your life? What sword of the Spirit can you apply? Comment on the power of exposure.

_____

_____

_____

_____

_____

A Course in Deliverance

God gave me the following dream when He was teaching me spiritual warfare.

I entered a very dark room from the back door. A black and white movie ran on a big screen television. Blue light lit the peoples' faces. As my eyes adjusted, I saw twenty people in different kinds of wheelchairs watching the movie. Some had head supports attached to their chairs. They had no power in any of their limbs. They were totally dependent on others to help them. Everyone was captivated by the show. I wasn't. I said to myself, "I'm not watching this." I wanted to leave by the side door, but if I did sunlight would pour in. The room was so dark that light would hurt their eyes. I have sensitive blue eyes. I know what it's like to come out from a dark space and be "blinded" by the light. It hurts! I usually close my eyes in reaction to the sunlight and then seriously squint until my eyes can adjust. I didn't want to cause these folks any pain. They certainly looked like they had enough trouble.

I didn't want to disturb their show. They really were enjoying it, though I sensed they had seen the same thing many times before. I also knew they would not appreciate the interruption. They would become belligerent if disturbed.

Then God said to me in the dream, "That's the problem. No one wants to disturb them. No one will shine light into the darkness." I realized they were immobilized, in darkness, and unable to help themselves. They were mesmerized by what they "watched" and had become comfortable under the spell.

It is possible for any one of us to be fooled by Satan. We need the Word of God, because people won't like the truth and we have to be so grounded in Scripture that it is more real than the temporary moral standards of our various societies.

11) How does Paul describe those who do not believe God's truth? (2Timothy 2:25,26) What attitude does the Word of God tell us to take? Why?

_____

_____

_____

_____

_____

_____

Bridge for Peace Foundation for Freedom

People can be careless about occult activities and become paralyzed by spirits of darkness. Many are convinced the supernatural is a joke, but some have been persuaded otherwise.

A man who had gone on a Peru tour came to a service for prayer. He visited their temples. He thought he would be funny and climbed up on an ancient sacrificial altar to a false god to have his photo taken. The demon took his offering seriously. He started to hear demons. He became sick. He couldn't function at his business anymore. Once a wealthy man, he lost everything.

12) Occult activity is often presented as a game or thought of as harmless. Talisman jewelry, garden statues of pagan gods, and horoscopes are stylish. How can you use the sword of the Spirit to guard yourself?

_____

_____

_____

_____

_____

Satan is aggressive. If he doesn't bother us, we don't often rush in to where he holds captives. But he takes advantage of every situation to gain power. He even pushes his way in when people are desperate for healing.

Arlene told me that her mother had died young and she experienced horrific family rejection. She sought comfort in relationships that compounded her pain. Continuously anxious, medical problems began to plague her. She had two episodes of precancerous situations that scared her. Arlene liked her doctor and felt she was competent and responsive to her concerns. "My doctor gave me a phone number and suggested I call this woman. She said this woman was very good and that she could definitely help me.

"I made inquiries. She was very expensive, but I figured this was serious. I pulled out the plastic and I called. She called herself a 'medical intuitive.' We had several phone appointments. She suggested I take some products, but they harmed my body. So I stopped. Next time we spoke she was really angry with me, because I stopped taking the products, which were also really expensive. She became very insistent that I resume. I resisted. She yelled

A Course in Deliverance

at me on the phone. I told her to calm down and then she shrieked, 'If you don't do exactly what I say then *you will get cancer! Do you hear me? You will get cancer!'* I felt a sword go through me. That night I felt possessed. I cried out, 'My God, my God please help me, I feel possessed.' What has come upon me? I'm doing things now that I would have thought were crazy."

The sword she felt go through her was not the sword of the Spirit. Satan has his sword as well. He has the counterfeit. After counseling with Arlene, our first step was to pray the *Covenant Prayer.* (See pg. 18) She rejected Satan and through the sword of the Spirit had strength to resist the harassing demons. The demons also resisted, but God is victorious. Arlene had a wonderful experience of God as she received the baptism of the Holy Spirit. She had a miraculous report about her health that encouraged her to persevere. Slowly, she reclaimed her inheritance. Victory is in Jesus Christ.

I often meet desperate people who seek help through witchdoctors with various titles. Some Christians are reluctant to believe in supernatural healing through Jesus Christ. Some don't want to talk about miracles. Satanic forces are ready to fill the vacuum these Christians leave. Satan's counterfeit healings ensnare people. He lies about death. Some believe they and their relatives will not die, but be "reincarnated."

In China, Ed and I went on a temple tour that consisted of a series of caves. The tour guide, a young woman, believed in reincarnation. Her family lived in one small room. As she showed us rock carvings that taught the reincarnation cycle she said, "My grandfather died. He used to live with us and we all miss him. I had a dream that he was very cold where he was. My family was worried. We bought a coat and some food for him. We burned the food so he could receive it in the "world" he was in." This family hardly had enough for themselves, yet they were burning food. We shared the good news with her. We were being watched by two men. She cautioned us and advised that the three of us should move on. Still, we shared whatever we could about Jesus and prayed for her as we went.

The bondage of Satan is cruel. A professional American lady, a church-goer, tormented by spirits of depression, asked me for prayer. She said, "I'm caught in a trap. I will do anything. I would gnaw off my arm like a trapped fox chews off its leg to get free." She went through the motions, raising her arm to her mouth. I pulled out the sword of the Spirit and quoted Psalm 91:3 He will rescue you from the trap of the hunter...." I praise God that before we finished praying together, this tormented lady experienced Christ's peace.

God told me, "Separate the living from the dead and then raise the dead." Desperate people create an anxious world. Some feel most alive when engaged in danger or when risking their own lives. They don't recognize their own despair, it feels normal. As Revelation 3:1 says, "...you have a reputation for being alive, but you are dead."

Bridge for Peace Foundation for Freedom

Many of us have deadened ourselves through our choices. Some don't know Christ, but acknowledge something bigger out there—a higher power, a benevolent universe. Some serve violent gods. Others call themselves God-haters. God knows those who appear alive, but are dead. He calls His servants to deliver them from death through the sword of the Spirit. Through the power of Christ's blood, we are called to raise the dead.

I pray God will use me as a sword in His hand to liberate people through His power. We are God's secret weapons, praying for the captive's liberation. He has concealed us in the shadow of His hand as He makes our mouths like sharpened swords. Through prayer we pierce the most profound darkness with the sword of the Spirit, and Christ's light shines through. (Isaiah 49:2)

13) Comment on God's role for you as a spiritual warrior.

_____

_____

_____

_____

_____

_____

Chapter 6
The Piercing Sword

Chapter Seven

Choose Life

God gives us days kissed with His favor, rich in love, and bursting with prosperity and serenity. He urges us to choose life by worshiping and serving Him. Of course, there is another choice. We choose death by exalting false gods, including self-absorption. The result is a dissatisfied heart, ears deaf to God's guidance, and curse following upon curse. God offers us two possibilities: life or death. (Deuteronomy 30:15-20)

We wonder why anyone would choose death. Don't underestimate Satan. He is an expert in making wrong choices look enticing.

A young woman told me, "I knew I would choose Jesus eventually, but I thought being a Christian would be boring. Now I've chosen Jesus and realize everything else is boring compared with life in Jesus!"

Talking with God, learning about His awesome wisdom and love through Scripture, and journeying with God's family is a great adventure. Knowing more and more how much we need Him and learning daily how God is totally for us brings a peace worldly security can never provide. Our Holy Spirit tutors us and guides us into an expansive life. God shows us how to be free. Through His supernatural power, He leads us into a wholeness that nothing and no one else can supply.

WE NEED OUR SAVIOR

Choosing life is choosing Jesus. Deliverance, turning from demonic spirits, coming free of the influence of Satan, this is choosing life. People addicted to drugs, alcohol, or other things know they need something. We help them to name the "something" we know is Jesus.

Once the need for a savior is realized, people readily accept Jesus Christ. Jonathan used drugs to cope with life. He said, "I know I need God. I believe in God, Jesus, and innumerable forces out there of good and evil. But, I know I don't pray as I should. I say, 'Jesus, if you'll help me get narcotics this time, I'll never use again.' I know you can't bargain with God, so that's not really a prayer. It's only a matter of time until I self-destruct."

Obviously, Jonathan knew about Jesus. It was what Jonathan did not know that became his downfall. He hadn't encountered Christ. Christ was merely one of many superior powers to him.

Bridge for Peace Foundation for Freedom

Jonathan, like many young people, had a strong sense of the spiritual realm, and a fascination with Buddhist meditation and the chanting in yoga classes that gave him a sense of peace. An online translation of the opening Sanskrit chant in Ashtanga Yoga follows: *I bow before the lotus feet of the Supreme Guru which awakens insight ... I prostrate myself before the sage Patanjali, who has thousands of radiant, white heads as the divine serpent, etc.*

Helping a person recognize Christ is not about winning or losing. It is about life and death.

Belief in strange gods is increasingly prevalent today. When you meet a person with these beliefs, do not become defensive. God does not need us to defend Him. Do not make it about you. Do not let Satan engage your ego. This is not your battle, but God's. God wants to use you as His instrument of deliverance. Helping a person recognize Christ is not about winning or losing. It is about life and death.

I hoped to stir up Jonathan's hunger for the authentic and make him angry with the Devil's destructive plot against him. I hoped to introduce him to Jesus.

Scripture verses, sometimes rephrased in my own words, help me to share truth. Listening for the Holy Spirit's guidance is imperative for me. Don't worry—if the Holy Spirit has something to tell you and you are listening closely, you will hear Gods voice. (For more on hearing God's voice, I recommend our CD *Dig in with God*.)

Ask questions. When we ask questions we show our concern and can understand people's perspectives. Listen to the speaker and to the Holy Spirit. Stay open to the Lord and speak what He puts in your heart. The Lord taught me this many years ago, as you can see from the following example.

I met a young woman, about 16 years of age, while I was walking a neighborhood on street ministry. The Lord said to me, "Keep her talking." As we walked together, I asked general questions and she revealed personal facts. I was out of my comfort zone. To keep her talking, my questions had to become personal. I felt like I was prying. It was very unnatural for me, but I was obeying God. She was perfectly at ease revealing family history and how her parents had abandoned her. She was living with a bunch of other kids. A warlock had gotten involved with them, which she thought was cool. She knew about Jesus, but the mystery of the occult was very enticing. She felt special, superior, being involved in a secret society. She was choosing death. Thank God a local pastor was willing to follow her up.

Jonathan said eventually he would "self-destruct." He was choosing death. I listened carefully and sought wisdom to share the right testimonies to bring him hope. When we prayed together I canceled negative words he had spoken over himself. He prayed to be delivered, recommitted himself to Christ, and was baptized in the Holy Spirit. He has achieved several milestones since choosing life. Slowly, he is moving ahead through Jesus.

A Course in Deliverance

Witnessing to God's power brings hope. Testimonies stir a desire to seek Jesus. God says, "If you seek Me you will find Me when you seek Me with all of your heart." (Jeremiah 29:13) I find that scripture reassuring. I pray God will use us to inspire people to seek Jesus, because I have no doubt that they will find Him.

1) The key to deliverance is the blood of Jesus Christ. We point people to Jesus and He saves. What does the Bible tell us we are to teach? (Read 1Timothy 4:10-11.)

_____

_____

_____

_____

_____

_____

We celebrate every victory, but do not underestimate the importance of vigilance in prayer. Demons want to satisfy their cravings through a human body and they look to re-enter.

A man in his thirties had an alcohol problem. He was instantly delivered through Jesus Christ. I emphasize the word instantly! Years later, he started the practice of drinking a glass of wine with dinner. He had a dream.

He saw a graveyard, and a skeleton's arm came up from the earth, the bony hand reaching for something. He had a sense it had to do with the spirit of alcohol and death reaching for him again. When God has delivered us, we need to be vigilant. Don't compromise or take grace for granted. Satan is on the prowl.

2) Can you identify a potentially vulnerable area in your life? What tools has God given you to remain vigilant? (Read 1Peter 5:8-10.) Discuss the tools in your group.

_____

_____

_____

THE SOLUTION TO EVERY PROBLEM

Eric struggled with drug addiction. He shared a vision that felt very real to him.

"I saw myself drowning. I called for help. My family was on the shore, but no one could hear me. I thrashed around and shouted for help, but they still couldn't hear me. I was so angry, I hated them because they didn't hear me and they never responded."

"Do you know this is a spiritual problem?" I asked.
"Absolutely," he replied.
"In the vision you call out horizontally to your family. Could you be calling out in the wrong direction? If this is a spiritual problem, human beings can't resolve it. If you've been saved from death many times, as you say, people must be praying for you and you've been protected."
"Yeah, I know that." He shared specific instances when he was certain prayer had preserved him.
"But, they can't hear the cry of your spirit or heal it. You are calling, 'Save me! Save me!' Only Jesus can do that. You're calling human beings, looking to them to save you, but you need to direct your cry vertically to God," I gestured heavenward.
"Yeah. That's it. That is exactly it."
"Jesus Christ is the only One Who can save you, that is why He's called Savior. You need a Savior." Eric was ready to choose life.

When someone shares a vision, I return to it, explore it, and ask questions. Eric's drowning scene was vivid. He felt the intense pain of not being heard in the midst of his crisis. Jesus Christ had to be revealed both as One who hears and as Savior. I was excited to share with Eric that Jesus made Himself known as *Savior*. That is the perfect name for a drowning person. A person who yells, "Save me!" knows their need for a Savior. Scripture says, "For there is born to you today, in David's city, a Savior, Who is Christ the Lord." (Luke 2:11)

Eric intuitively knew the core of his problem was spiritual. He agreed he needed a spiritual solution. He needed God.

Eric thought God was too busy taking care of the universe to be concerned about his problems, a common erroneous belief. I had to address two points with Eric. First, the family's powerful prayers had shown their love and involvement. Their intercession had been key to his survival. Secondly, God was always intimately involved in his daily life.

AGREEMENT AND UNITY

Eric acknowledged that supernatural intervention caused him to survive many altercations, car accidents, and drug incidents. He knew his avoidance of more serious consequences had to have been the result of prayer. This gave me opportunity to remind him that his family loved him.

A Course in Deliverance

Prayer requires a caring heart. Prayer takes time. I stressed his family's investment of prayer and the benefits he had reaped from it. Eric acknowledged this was true. I wanted his agreement before we went any further.

Lies had to be confronted and a new foundation had to be laid. I wanted him to recognize his family's love. He agreed that his family had done what they could and had prayed for him. Instructing Eric through Scripture and waiting for his agreement began to tear down strongholds. An instructive verse regarding the influence of intercession is, "The insistent prayer of a righteous person is powerfully effective." (James 5:16b) We read this together. The Holy Spirit shifted Eric's perspective from resentment of his family to gratitude for their prayerful insistence and the power it released.

Teach, testify, and tell the good news.

Listening for agreement as you move forward in deliverance is important. You can't proceed further than the agreement given. You are laying a foundation, brick by brick. You can't skip any steps. Get the agreement as you build. Teach, testify, and tell the good news. If you don't get agreement, pray and battle. You need the "yes." I refer you to Cynthia's story in Chapter 5. She stopped agreeing. When she said, "no," the demon had exposed itself and it was time to change tactics.

The following is a dream I had that shows consequences of disunity in the body of Christ.

I dreamt I walked on the beach with a young woman in her twenties. She was excited to try the latest thing that everyone was doing. (This was a dream, where impossibilities appear normal.) *Young people shrunk themselves very small by willpower. They squeezed themselves into colored glass bottles and floated out to sea. I tried to dissuade her. She did it anyway. The tide was going out, the sun had set, and she was drifting somewhere on the sea. I ran into the knee deep water and picked up the glass bottles searching for her to free her before it was too late. I released young men and women. Some bottles had whole families in them that I released. But I couldn't find this young woman.*

So many bottles were drifting! The sky grew darker, night was coming. People had come down to enjoy the close of the day at the beach. They stood near the shoreline. They strolled on the sand. "Help!" I called out to them. Swiftly, I explained that people were drifting. Soon it would be dark and impossible to see. Black clouds moved in from the horizon. The bottled people would be swept out to sea on the tide and lost forever.

The shore people agreed to help. They discussed how to help, but couldn't decide on the method to use. They weighed the possible pros and cons of each suggestion. I was desperate, grabbing all the bottles I could, freeing people. I could hear the discussion onshore. Though the situation was critical, the people who wanted to help and saw the real need disagreed with one another dispassionately, as though deciding on white bread or rye. They fully intended to help, but had no sense of urgency in the matter.

If you are praying with a deliverance team, unity is imperative. Christ tells us agreement has power. (Matthew 18:19) Discord is Satan's realm. If unity and submission to God is not present on a deliverance team a great deal of damage can be done. Satan promotes egotism. If we allow our vanity to get involved he will put on a show at the expense of the demonized person.

We observed a disastrous fiasco when a controlling person assumed leadership of a team praying for deliverance. The demon was stubborn. The situation escalated into a battle of wills. The demonized woman suffered and God's glory was being robbed.

When we became aware of what was happening, the B4P team waited for Ed to act. He thanked the other prayer ministers and the crowd watching and told them to go home. He stood there, gracious, patient, and firm until everyone had complied. Within moments, the person who had struggled for well over an hour was delivered by the B4P team. Ed acted as God's ambassador. Motivated by compassion, he exerted authority and demonstrated God's power. God was glorified.

3) What does the Bible say about unity? Why is unity essential in deliverance ministry? (Read Psalm 133.)

_____

_____

_____

_____

_____

_____

HIGH ABOVE OUR WAYS

Eric agreed he had a spiritual problem and God was the solution. But Eric lacked instruction on the nature of God. People often say God is too busy running the universe to think about helping them. We tend to recreate God in our own image. "Too busy" is a common denominator in western societies. His ways are very different from ours. The Word says they are "higher." (Isaiah 55: 8-9) The Bible gives an example of how wide the difference is

A Course in Deliverance

between our ways and His. It says, "...as the heavens are higher than the earth, so are My ways higher than your ways."

A scientist estimated the distance between the heavens and the earth. He named the point where our solar system ended as the beginning of the heavens. He arrived at 33,968 trillion miles as the measurement. I remember when Ed received his million miler air travel card. A million miles boggled my mind! God's pure and holy ways are over 33,968 trillion miles different from what seems normal to us.

God is everywhere in the same moment, knows everything, and is ultimate power. I wanted Eric to feel reassured by this, rather than frightened or guilty that God was watching him. I hoped to convey God's security, love, and protection available to him. The good news was that God was intensely interested in him. God was willing and able to save him from destructive patterns. He wanted to hear from Eric and talk with him. "...casting all your worries on Him, because He cares for you." (1Peter 5:7)

4) Can you share a testimony of how God showed His loving care for you?

_____

_____

_____

_____

_____

_____

JESUS THE TRUE FRIEND

Craig was deeply involved with drugs. As we spoke, he moved to the edge of his seat, as though discovering something exciting. The Holy Spirit stirred him. "The spiritual forces, Jesus, the higher power, whoever," he gestured wildly with his arms, "are there for good. But I always listen to this other one on my shoulder." He turned and looked at his left shoulder as though someone was perched there. "I've befriended it." Craig made friends with a demonic spirit that wanted to destroy him. He had chosen death.

"There *is* someone on your shoulder," I responded. "That's real. It says it is your friend. It's lying. It's a destructive spirit. As you say, there are different forces. But there is only one Jesus; one true God Who is Light. And the others, whether called by the name of a god or a satanic name, are forces of darkness. They pretend to be your friend, but what they do is insist, demand, and plan to control you. Forces of darkness bring constant pressure into your life." Sometimes, as noted earlier in this chapter, the first need is to expose the lie of many good gods. Jesus Christ is the true friend who could free Craig. We discussed Jesus Christ as the only true God, our Triune God—Father, Son, and Holy Spirit. After sharing Scripture and experience, agreement followed that Jesus Christ and only Jesus Christ is Lord. I could see revelation come to Craig through the Holy Spirit. He began to understand that Jesus Christ is the true friend.

I like to speak Scripture conversationally, as well as reading the Bible with the person in need. Sometimes, I'll turn to a verse and invite the person to read it. I have found that practice very effective in breaking down lies in people's minds and restoring hope. In this case, I did not want to break eye contact. I shared Scripture as we talked together. That was what I sensed was appropriate at the time. Do not be rigid, but rely on the Holy Spirit.

A helpful scripture is: "Therefore God also highly exalted Him, and gave to Him the name which is above every name, that at the name of Jesus every knee should bow, of those in heaven, those on earth, and those under the earth, and that every tongue should confess that Jesus Christ is Lord, to the glory of God the Father." (Philippians 2:9-11) This scripture exalts Christ and portrays Satan's position.

5) When a person is confused, the sword of the Spirit which is the Word of God is a powerful tool to bring clarity. What favorite scripture may help you teach Christ's sovereignty over Satan?

_____

_____

_____

_____

_____

UNMASKED

There was something sitting on Craig's shoulder. He could sense it, spoke to it, and was often directed by it. I remembered an elderly gentleman in Australia refer to Satan as "Old Nick on my shoulder." I had never thought of the Devil sitting on someone's shoulder. I asked

A Course in Deliverance

about the title and was told it was just an expression, but it is more than that. Experience has shown me people do sense demons on their back and on their shoulder. Craig's very real description reminded me that other people in Australia had his same experience many years ago. Like Craig, they had demons on their shoulders speaking to them.

I knew Craig sensed realities in the spirit realm. I affirmed him and helped bring clarity to his experience. We talked until he realized a dark spirit was coaching him. This was not just a vague sense, but a demonic personality. I reminded him how he had befriended it. No one would befriend an evil monster, but Scripture tells us that, "Satan himself masquerades as an angel of light." (2Corinthians 11:14)

I explained to Craig how Satan intended to deceive him. He didn't present himself as wicked, but as a friend. I explained to Craig that Satan hated him because of the opportunity he had through Jesus Christ. "Satan once walked on the heights of heaven. He knows the beauty. He knows the glory. And he knows he will *never* walk there again, but you can walk in heaven one day through Jesus Christ.

"Satan hates you. He badgers you, gives you all the reasons why you should use drugs, then accuses you for taking them. He never stops. He wants to destroy you. The perfect love you are looking for is found in your Father God, His Son Jesus, and the Holy Spirit. Jesus stands and invites you; He speaks softly, but with the power of love."

6) Give an example of how Satan masquerades as an angel of light. In this situation, how can you expose him?

_____

_____

_____

_____

_____

THE STILL SMALL VOICE

God's amazing intervention became plain! Craig looked over his right shoulder as he spoke. "This light and goodness actually outweighs the darkness. It's more powerful, but it feels like a feather. It feels light." He sensed the presence of God! Craig turned again toward his left side. "I want to just push this darkness off my shoulder."

"But you can't. You need Jesus to do it. This is what the victory of the cross is about."
"That's what I need. That's truth. It makes a lot of sense. I help a lot of people. Yet I can't help myself. I always wonder why I can't help myself." He said, "I want to reject it."

His use of the word "reject" alerted me. It was the same word B4P prays in our *Covenant Prayer.* The word "reject" is used in churches to renew baptismal vows. "Do you reject Satan and all his empty promises...?" This was my time to move. He was ready not only to reject Satan, but to accept Jesus.

I encouraged Craig. "Why don't you do that right now? Just tell that spirit of darkness on your shoulder that it is not your friend. You don't want it. You reject it."
"I reject you. You're not my friend."

Don't hesitate, procrastinate, or meditate. Move.

Never, never delay. When you sense the time is now, plunge in. Don't hesitate, procrastinate, or meditate. Move. The Holy Spirit is directing, be direct. This is the anointed moment. Don't imagine it will come again later. Optimize it. Get the job done. I cannot stress the importance of moving the very moment you know the Spirit has brought revelation. Glory be to God. He alone sets the captive free! God will direct you to play your part, don't be anxious. Just do it! Jesus tells us to be as shrewd as snakes and as innocent as doves. (Matthew 10:16) Be perceptive and seize the opening. Bring them into God's strong tower, safe from the enemy. (Psalm 61:3)

Whatever words you need to speak in the moment of deliverance, you can do it. God put *you* there. He wants to work through *you*. At this particular moment of deliverance, when God has positioned the event, you might tell a story. It is a time to be direct, in *your* way. Remember, God is using you to help a drowning person call out to the Savior. God is leading you. He arranged the whole scenario. Satan didn't arrange it, believe me. Don't get hung up now, the Devil doesn't want you going forward at this moment. He will bring insecurities, uncertainties, and make you self-conscious if he can. Do it your way, but do it. The person needs to reject Satan and accept Jesus. All heaven is on your side and the power of God is with you. Speak the words.

7) Jesus understands the power of the Devil. He gave all authority to you in His name to lead people to the truth and help them escape. (Read 2Timothy 2:25-26.) Satan will try to make you believe you are inadequate. What could help you grow in holy boldness? Share ideas.

A Course in Deliverance

_____

_____

_____

_____

_____

A friend just said to Ed and me, "I was talking with someone at work. They had a bad headache and another co-worker was offering them some pain relief medication. I wanted to tell them about Jesus and His healing power, but I couldn't seem to do it. The next day, I was on the golf course, someone had a leg problem. I wanted to pray for them, but I couldn't seem to get there." He was really frustrated.

Ed said, "Why don't you tell a story, just like we do on the healing line? I prayed for someone who had," Ed waved his hand, "whatever is relevant. And I saw...whatever healing you saw." He lit up. "I can do that! Yeah, I can do that!"
Next time we met I asked, "How are you doing?"
"Great, I just prayed for someone in the supermarket."

You can do this. You can minister deliverance. God told us to set the captive free.

8) A lady told me she wasn't afraid of the Devil, but she was afraid of "doing deliverance wrong." Do you now or have you had concerns like hers? Do you have any apprehension about "doing deliverance wrong?" Share with your group. If studying on your own feel free to contact B4P with any questions you might still have after completing the next chapter.

_____

_____

_____

_____

_____

_____

Paul had chosen death. He said he had recently taken drugs and had a lot to lose if it was discovered. He was being monitored, but hoped the chemical wouldn't be detected.

"You like to take risks?" I asked.

"Yes, that's exactly it. Something inside me says I can get away with it. That's why I do it. Challenge the system."

"Like an adventure?"

"Yeah. Something in me says, 'Why not? You can get away with it, others can't.'"

"Something makes it sound adventurous; meanwhile, that something is a someone and he plans to destroy you. That's what Jesus told us. Demons will torment you and pressure you to choose destruction. If Satan approached you with his face contorted with hatred and rage you would not listen to anything he suggested. He knows this and he is sly. That is why he comes in a form you will accept. He makes destructive behavior look like an adventure. He appeals to your vanity urging, 'You can do it. Everyone else may get caught, but you'll get away with it.' When we act on his suggestion, then he begins his torturous name-calling and degradation."

Keep your eyes open when you pray.

Paul's voice sounded distant as he said, "I saw myself once. Six foot down in the earth. I was lying there giving my own eulogy. I was saying things like, 'I was addicted to drugs and alcohol. I brought pain to a lot of people'. It was terrible."

"That is what the spirits of darkness have planned for you."

"I know it," he exhaled.

"Jesus said, 'The thief only comes to steal, kill, and destroy.' (John10:10) Jesus specifically mentions destruction. Satan is the thief. He says it will work out, but it works into deeper darkness and ultimately total destruction–death. Your hopes and dreams die, relationships, and the ultimate plan is to kill your body and possess your soul."

I could see Paul was struggling. He was agitated in his seat. Uncomfortable realities confronted him. He was re-evaluating his decision. Jesus would bring him through.

Watching body language is very important in deliverance ministry. Keep your eyes open when you pray. Sometimes people twitch. This can be either the power of God or a demonic manifestation. Keep your eye on them. If it is a demonic manifestation, they could lose control. Be prepared. Features can become contorted or an expression of pain can cross their face. Sometimes, they reach for a talisman concealed in a pocket. Attentive listening, responding as the Holy Spirit leads, and asking questions are all tools. Let the Holy Spirit guide you and reveal truth to you. When I see the light of revelation and hope in the person's face, I move on to the next issue.

A man on the prayer line told me, "You prayed for me last year. I'm not afraid of myself anymore. Since you prayed for me, I'm free. I pray this prayer every day. Can I share it with you?"

A Course in Deliverance

"Sure," I responded. He took out several typed pages and began to read, repenting of various sexual sins. I asked to see the list, skimmed it, and handed it back. I didn't want to hear it read out loud. It named many depraved spirits. I said, "Friend, you have been freed by Jesus Christ. Now let's give Him the glory. Think of a prayer that would say, 'Thank you, Jesus. I am free now because of Your blood and resurrection power. This prayer recalls who you were, not who you are. This prayer keeps your memory of sin alive."

"Oh. So I should say, 'Thank you Jesus for delivering me? Thank you Jesus for healing me?"

"Perfect!"

Demonic spirits foster self-loathing and then suggest suicide. Discourage rehashing the past and self-criticism that could absolutely become an opening for new temptation. Encourage praising God with gratitude.

9) What did you find particularly helpful in this chapter?

_____

_____

_____

_____

_____

Chapter Eight

Delivered

THE INHERITANCE RESPONSE

Grabbing threatening snakes by the tail, producing God-fruit, demolishing strongholds, unmasking Satan, wielding the sword of the Spirit...we have travelled great roads together thanks to Jesus Christ. In this last chapter, we return to the inheritance Christ has purchased for us—salvation, healing, deliverance, and provision—our precious treasure at the center of the spiritual battle. Spiritual histories demonstrate the role of the spirit of death in robbing the inheritance from the rightful owner.

We will study three inheritance fights beginning with Jacob and Esau in 2,000 BC. Brothers wrangle over the family fortune and one plots murder. Over one thousand years later, we read another case of inherited property threatened by authority. King Ahaz and his wife Jezebel fall prey to the jealously, envy, and greed that lurk in the shadows of spiritual darkness. They want the inheritance of their subject, Naboth, who insists he will preserve it. A bloody murder settles the question. Nearly another thousand years pass and Jesus teaches about inheritance, covetousness, and mob mentality.

VULNERABLE

Jacob and Esau are two brothers with very different personalities who failed to appreciate the difference. Esau, the firstborn and rugged outdoorsman, was favored by his father, Isaac. Jacob, the stay-at-home, was the cherished child of his mother, Rebekah.

Esau would inherit the family fortune as the oldest and would be expected to take his wealthy father's position of patriarch. However God had said Esau would serve Jacob. Rebekah knew the prophecy. Her husband Isaac had grown old. Her boys were men now. Rebekah plotted to ensure the prophecy would come to pass. The full extent of her influence on Jacob is unknown. Did she unintentionally or deliberately reveal the prophecy? Did she taunt Esau, pleased that he would be subservient to his brother? Did she fuel the competition between her two sons? Is that what led to the scene around the campfire?

Jacob knelt, stirring the fragrant lentils spiced with garden herbs and vegetables. Esau, hauling home after the hunt, smelled the stew as he lurched toward the family compound. His mouth watered in anticipation of devouring a steaming bowlful. Covered in sweat, he broke the clearing and collapsed next to his brother's cook fire.

"Give me some," Esau barked, his squinting eyes fixed on the pot. "I'm starving!" Involuntarily, he gulped as if already swallowing a great mouthful.

Jacob languidly lifted a ladle of lentils and poured them back into the pot, causing the rich aroma to rise and allowing Esau to see the pungent heartiness of his blend. He dipped again, raised the ladle to his lips and slurped, releasing a satisfied sigh as he returned to stirring the pot. Jacob's opportunity had come at last. His every move was calculated to entice Esau. His heart was full of cunning, even as Esau's was filled with contempt.

Jacob replied casually, "First, give me your birthright." His hooded eyes watched the pot, but tension gripped every bit of him like a thief about to seize a coveted prize.

"I'm dying here," Esau snarled, "what good will any birthright do me now!" He grabbed for the ladle.

Jacob hunched his shoulder and dodged him, "Swear. Swear to me first."

Esau spat, "I *swear!*"

Jacob's lips curled in a sly smile as he handed over the stew.

Esau threw his head back and poured full ladles into his mouth as the liquid ran down his bearded face.

Esau exaggerated his need. He certainly would not die of hunger on the spot. He wanted immediate satisfaction. He gave everything away for instantaneous gratification.

Satan watches us. He listens when we complain. He can't read our minds but, like a fox, he guesses our next move from patterns he has observed in our behavior. He calculates our level of perceived desperation. Like Esau, who claimed he would die without satisfying his hunger instantaneously, we can become desperate to satisfy a need. Satan measures our vulnerability, our willingness to accept his suggestion. At the opportune moment, he offers us a counterfeit—if we will trade our inheritance. What Satan offers will never fulfill us. His counterfeits produce a deeper dissatisfaction and desperation in his captives to fill their emptiness with whatever temporary fix he can supply.

Esau gives away his inheritance of his own free will, but he is tricked out of his father's final blessing. Esau realizes what he has given away of his own free will and the blessing that has been snatched from him by his brother's deception. Esau rages at Jacob. Esau threatens Jacob with murder to regain his inheritance, but it is too late. (Genesis 25:29-34, 27:41).

A Course in Deliverance

1) Where is your vulnerable area? This is a personal question that is not intended for group discussion.

_____

_____

_____

_____

_____

_____

2) Satan is after your inheritance. When we are tired, hungry, or frustrated we are more susceptible to temptations. Under what circumstances are you more likely to give in to the suggestion to complain, become unjustifiably angry or indulge self-pity, negating the reality of God's provision for you? What helps?

_____

_____

_____

_____

_____

_____

DETERMINED

A breeze drew Ahab, King of Samaria, to his palace window where he saw an enchanting scene. Dense grapevines climbed trellises and provided shade. Clusters of purple fruit dangled.

Their sweet fragrance scented the air, while birds sang sweetly in the vineyard, delighting the moody King Ahab. He imagined himself lounging in the soothing shade at noontime. And what a convenient vegetable garden the fertile ground could be, so close to the palace. He would have it at any cost.

The king contacted his neighbor, Naboth. Ahab proposed a trade for a better vineyard in his possession or a cash transaction if Naboth preferred. Naboth knew Ahab's viciousness. His ruthless reputation preceded him. Naboth might have asked for a few days to think it over. He could have bought himself some time to figure it out, but no. Naboth responded immediately. "God forbid I should give you my ancestral inheritance!"

Naboth knew opposing Ahab could bring retribution. Ahab had a reputation for vengeance and his wife Jezebel was notorious. Naboth valued his inheritance so dearly that he was willing to take whatever retaliation the conniving couple imposed on him. No one would take his inheritance from him and it was not for sale. Before Ahab asked, Naboth had already decided he would guard his inherited vineyard at any cost. Because of Naboth's refusal Jezebel used her influence to have him murdered on trumped up charges. After Naboth was mercilessly stoned, Jezebel and Ahab stole Naboth's inheritance. (1Kings 21:1-16)

3) Compare Esau and Naboth. Have you made up your mind concerning your inheritance in Christ? Are you determined to guard it? Discuss.

_____

_____

_____

_____

_____

_____

THE HEIR

Jesus told a parable (Mark 12:1-12). A landowner plants a vineyard and builds a fence around it to protect it. He digs into the earth, preparing a place for the winepress. He constructs a tower to safeguard the property. He travels to distant parts and puts all of his work into the hands of others to tend and harvest. They will be rewarded when the harvest is brought in. The season is ripe and the landowner sends a representative to collect his share of the harvest. The tenants decide they want it all. They abuse the man and send him away with nothing. The landlord sends another representative and they beat him and treat him shamefully. Again the landlord sends out a servant—they murder him. He continues to send men and the tenants continue to murder them. Finally, the landlord sends his beloved son thinking the tenants will respect him. "But those tenants said to one another, 'This is the heir. Come, let's kill him and the inheritance will be ours!'" They seized him and killed him. (Mark 12:7)

We are now the heirs. Demons scheme to treat us shamefully. They want our inheritance. Thievery, violence, murder—whatever it takes—brazen demonic spirits storm through resistance to grab our legacy in Christ. Like a vice-grip they apply force expecting us to crack and turn from Christ. Because of our ignorance, spirits of infirmity easily violate the boundary Christ established in 1Peter 2:24, "through His bruises you have been healed." Rebellious demons test and prod for entryways into our hearts and minds. If we don't know they are illegal, we seek human help for spiritual problems and in despair decide we have to "learn to live with it," whatever problem plagues us. Finally, we let Satan rob us of Christ's peace, prosperity, and even life itself.

4) You have been chosen, adopted, and given an inheritance in Christ. You understand Satan's contempt and endless attempts to inflict misery and destruction on you and all human kind. Christ has fulfilled every promise He has made you. He has given you an inheritance. You have knowledge, which is power. What does Christ ask of you? What response do you make?

_____

_____

_____

_____

_____

RESSURECTION POWER

Christ shows us that Satan maneuvers to kill the heir. He sends out spirits of suicide and death to accomplish his will. According to worldatlas.com, between 1970-2015 suicide rates worldwide rose 60%. Obviously, that does not include attempted suicides. The United States

Bridge for Peace Foundation for Freedom

Center for Disease Control and Prevention lists suicide as the second leading cause of death for those aged 15-34. The third leading cause of death in that same age group is homicide. We thank God for psychiatrists and all mental health professionals. Thank God for medical testing that discovers chemical imbalances, food allergies, and other problems. Praise God for all helpful medications. May the medical community continue to do their job, helping people in need.

Our work is praying for those who need the supernatural power available from Christ's cross and resurrection.

However, we as the Christian community must do our part. Our work is praying for those who need the supernatural power available from Christ's cross and resurrection.

Unaware of what Christ offers, ignorant of our inheritance in Him, naive about the spiritual battle, we are easy prey for demonic spirits. Satan will exploit us—unless we are ready to battle.

Years ago, the spirit of suicide revealed itself to me. It then tried to silence me, to keep me from freeing others. Satan seriously miscalculated. Thank you Jesus, I give You all the glory!

In 2008, Ed and I were in the midst of building the healing center. Pressures were enormous, but the vision we waited for was being fulfilled. I was s-t-r-e-t-c-h-e-d! We expected challenges to arise but they exceeded our imaginations. We knew Jesus would show us how to work them through. Without exaggeration, God showed us miracles of administration nearly every single day. Bridge for Peace continued to grow and with it came the trials of expansion.

One night we had a wondrous healing prayer service at a local church. It was a great night with the Bridge for Peace team. Everyone who had a need received from God. God demonstrated His miracle-working power and some received baptism in the Spirit. Ed and I had separate cars. I traveled home, tired but fulfilled. Ed and I were experiencing new heights in the Lord, and Satan wanted to throw me down. He wanted to finish Bridge for Peace now, before we could do more damage to his kingdom through radical obedience to Christ.

I heard in my head, "Why don't you end it all now?" I was confused. The voice repeated, "Why don't you end it all now?" While I was still processing this, the voice said, "Where are all the people you helped who said they would be there to help you? Where are all the people who were healed?"

I realized it was the Devil who spoke to me. I answered, "Whatever I did, I did for Jesus."

A Course in Deliverance

"But where are the men whose wives were healed, those men who said, 'You've changed my family's lives.' Those people who said they were grateful, but never did anything to show any gratitude. Where are they now when you need help?" The voice was very compelling.

"Everything I've done has been in obedience to Jesus. I'm not expecting anything from men."

"Why don't you drive into the lake now and end it all?"

And then the demonic spirit left me. Angels guarded me.

I told Ed later, "Suicide is a *spirit*. It *spoke* to me." I met the spirit of suicide. The *nerve* of that Devil! I became angry at the Devil after I thought about my experience. Anger was not my first response. Though Satan's suggestion was outrageous, it appeared through supernatural demonic power to have merit in the moment. Don't underestimate the power of a satanic spell. Understand that satanists perform ceremonies to curse and destroy Christians. The first above-ground organized satanic church in America was founded in 1966 with international headquarters in New York.

Analyzing the temptation, I find the lying spirit tried to build resentment in me. First, Satan comes with a half-truth. It is true. Some people say they appreciate what Bridge for Peace has done for them, realize the need Bridge for Peace has, say they will help, but don't keep their word. Satan had that right. I am sure all Christian leaders have the same story. Ed and I have had plenty of experience with failed promises, so we cultivate a "wait and see" attitude. The half-truth was people failed, but the full truth is the whole premise Satan presented was rotten.

Jesus shows us the right attitude in His Word. Jesus said when I finished doing everything He told me to do, I should say, "'I am your unworthy servant, I have only done my duty.'" (Luke 17:10)

Serving Jesus is a privilege. Looking for a reward from men for obeying God is vile. Christ said we should beware of people who like to be honored and receive respect from men when fulfilling their duty to God. (Luke 20:46)

Jesus said those who love to be seen by others and praised by them have already received their reward. But those who serve for love of Him can look to Him for their reward. (Matthew 6:5-6)

Satan tried to build on unfulfilled promises made by men, but the premise that men should reward us for obeying God was a lie in itself.

5) Remember, a half-truth is a lie. Satan often comes with an ungodly premise and makes it appear rational, but God's ways are high above our ways. Has Satan told you a half-truth and convinced you it is legitmate?

_____

_____

_____

_____

_____

_____

Other temptations we can identify in this scenario include discouragement, self-pity, unrighteous anger, pride, self-importance and more. Satan was trying all of my doorknobs, but God blocked the entryway.

After I met the spirit of suicide, the Holy Spirit began to teach me through Scripture about Satan's ways. The Word says the Devil brought Jesus Christ to Jerusalem and stood Him on the highest point of the temple. At the highest corner of the temple, reports a historian of the period, was a precipice of dizzying heights. He says one could not see the bottom. Today, it is estimated as a 450 foot drop.

Satan tells Jesus to jump. If Jesus would have jumped, it would have been suicide. Jesus was tempted by the spirit of suicide. It's written in the Bible. There is no shame in being tempted. Jesus destroyed all shame, but Satan wants everyone tempted by suicide to be ashamed.

Preaching in a church one night, I felt led by the Holy Spirit to share my encounter with the spirit of suicide. I don't know why I was surprised when Satan began to speak to me again. "Don't tell everybody that...." He tried to make me ashamed, to be silent on the matter. I thought about it for maybe six seconds and said, "In the name of Jesus, go."

Satan is not a comic figure. Satan is cunning. Satan will appear to be your friend. Satan comes like an angel of light. When Satan makes a suggestion it seems to be in your best interest. Did I want to reveal these private thoughts and temptations to strangers? What might they think?

Since that encounter and revelation, Christ uses me to expose and deliver people from spirits of suicide. I've met pastors, priests, and ministers struggling daily with suicide. They were

A Course in Deliverance

ashamed to tell anyone and suffered isolation and depression. Jesus said He took all of our shame. How great He is to share with us about the suicide and other spirits that tempted Him so we could be free of shame.

6) As you read Luke 4:1-13, what do you notice about Christ's response and/or about Satan and his temptations?

_____

_____

_____

_____

_____

Note that I was not depressed when the spirit of suicide tempted me. Ed and I were under a great deal of pressure, but we were excited about what God was doing. It is not only the depressed who are tempted by the spirit of suicide.

Jesus Christ had just been filled with the power of the Holy Spirit. The Spirit led Him to the desert where He had a special time with His Father. The Word says Jesus felt the pressure of hunger, but it doesn't say Jesus was depressed.

I met a pastor who had been a Broadway actor. When he hit the height of his acting career, Satan tempted him. He had reached the top, what was left to live for? He now helps others find Jesus in their despair.

I met another former actor. This young man was a handsome platinum blonde, with a fit upper body. One night after taking cocaine, he climbed a tree. A voice suggested he could fly. He jumped. He's in a wheelchair today with crippled legs and a hopeless medical prognosis. He was furious at God. I pray for him now and hope he has found his way to Jesus. The temptation to jump or to fly is an old one. Jesus heard a similar voice.

I prayed for a doctor who had an international career. He is now a seminarian. He had a luxurious lifestyle and, in his words, "was involved in sin...." He lived in a high-rise apartment with a balcony overlooking the city. One night a force pressed him through the open doors to the balcony. It pressed him to the edge of the rail. Terrified, he called out to God, repented, and his life turned totally around.

When Satan stood Jesus on the high point of the temple, he misquoted Scripture to Him. Satan intentionally omitted a phrase and misrepresented Psalm 91:11-12. Satan told Jesus to jump, after all the Word says God will give His angels charge over You. The full passage says God will send angels to accompany, defend, and preserve us in all of our ways on the road *of obedience and service to God.* Satan knows Scripture and he will twist it for his own purposes. Jumping off the precipice would not be obedience to God; jumping would be obedience to Satan.

A woman pastor told me she had been tormented by thoughts of suicide for years. As I spoke on my experiences with that spirit, the spirit of suicide revealed itself to her. It hovered right before her face, close and threatening. She described its ugly face. She said, "I never knew it was a spirit. I have been so ashamed." She showed me her wrists where she had tattooed butterflies to cover the scars. I said, "You overcame, just as Jesus overcame. You have nothing to be ashamed of. His victory is in you."

7) What difference does it make when you realize suicide is a spirit?

_____

_____

_____

_____

_____

_____

Rebuke the spirit of suicide and the spirit of death the same way you rebuke any demonic spirit. Command it to go in the name of Jesus by the power of His blood. I recommend my CD *Power for Living* for more on this subject.

Satan tempted Jesus to bow down to him (C. Williams translates the Greek tense as "just once"). Satan offered Jesus a reward from choice treasures the world could give. If we accept Satan's twisted premises, we bow down to him. Certainly he will tell us we only have to do it once, but he's a liar. When we give ourselves to him he will not willingly release us. He will most certainly offer us temporary worldly rewards, plus unlimited curses. Jesus rebuked Satan by quoting Scripture, Jesus would worship the Lord and serve only Him. (Deuteronomy 6:16) Satan challenged Jesus saying, "If you are the Son of God...." Satan may tempt you by saying,

A Course in Deliverance

"If you are who you say you are, then…." In essence, he is taunting you, "Prove it…prove it!" You don't have anything to prove to Satan. (Luke 4:9-13)

Many people come for prayer when they realize suicide is a spirit. I pray for them, but often sense that through their new knowledge of God's Word they have already been delivered and taken back their inheritance. The blindness that kept them ashamed is gone.

8) Some people are bound by the spirit of shame. What is the key to their freedom?

_____

_____

_____

_____

_____

_____

FROM DEATH TO LIFE

Joan came for prayer. As the B4P team member prayed for Joan she slumped against her in an unresponsive state.

That night I had preached about the power of Christ's cross and resurrection to deliver us from spirits of death. A spirit of death takes many forms, as discussed in Chapter Six.

Despite deliverance commands in the name of Jesus, I was advised that Joan remained in the same condition. I went to assist the team member. Praying for Joan, I traced the cross on her forehead. This was not a method of deliverance. I don't remember ever doing that before, but the Holy Spirit must have instructed me. The demonic spirit in Joan thrashed her arms, kicked me, grabbed fistfuls of my clothes, and gnashed her teeth. Strong young men rushed to hold her down. We spoke the name of Jesus and released the power of His blood. She was delivered.

Through Christ's resurrection power, Joan crossed over from death to life. She prayed the *Covenant Prayer*, gave her life to Jesus, and was baptized in the Holy Spirit. (John 5:24)

117

Satan fears Jesus Christ. (Matthew 8:29) The Holy Spirit leads us in delivering the captive in the name of Jesus. Rely on the Holy Spirit, not your own wisdom. Do not fear the spirit of death. You are Christ's ambassador and Christ has authority over the Devil.

9) What does Colossians 2:15 say? Comment.

_____

_____

_____

_____

_____

_____

THE DAY THE DEMONS SHRIEKED

A B4P mission team served at a three day healing and deliverance conference in Brazil. On the first day, the men on the team said they had to avert their eyes because women dressed so inappropriately. We noticed talismans around people's necks. Drug abuse, murder, and thievery plagued the area. Violence was commonplace. Many who asked for prayer told terrible stories of witchcraft and domestic abuse.

As a team, we decided to have a deliverance service the next day. I opened my computer and the team composed a prayer. We listed the demonic spirits the Holy Spirit brought to mind when we prayed.

The next day, God prepared B4P. The team stationed themselves around the auditorium, ready to deal with demonic manifestations. My translator, a powerful servant of God, stood beside me. I heard the Holy Spirit say, "Don't start until people are seated and silent."

The people wandered in, kids ran in the bleachers, groups of people chatted. God said, "Wait." I asked everyone to take a seat. "We will begin when everyone is seated and quiet." I saw a commotion at the side door. A television crew arrived. Ed took them outside. I waited. It was getting uncomfortable, but I was not budging until we had silence. Some of the team said later, "I was thinking, 'Let's get on with it.'" Pressure mounted as time passed—the demands of the schedule, people's expectations, etc. But I also sensed God's anointing increasing. When you hear from God, resist every pressure, obey Him.

A Course in Deliverance

Finally, it was still and we began. On and on we went, rebuking and binding depraved spirits of darkness. If the Holy Spirit brought to mind other demons to anyone on the B4P team, we took authority over them in the name of Jesus. Forty minutes later the people in the auditorium still sat in silence. Not one single manifestation occurred.

At the break, Kevin asked if anyone heard the screaming outside the building. I had heard it in the upper left side of the auditorium. I thought fans were sitting high on the bleachers outside, yelling for their team at a sports match. No one else heard it.

Our local coordinator went outside and walked around the building. "There's only an alleyway out there. There is no sports field or playground anywhere out there."

The next day women showed up in modest dress. The entire atmosphere of the meeting changed. Many testified to deliverance.

We realized there had not been a single manifestation of deliverance, yet so many had been set free through Jesus Christ. We couldn't measure the results, but we agreed that to say God delivered hundreds that day is not an exaggeration. The demons shrieked on their way out, that's what two of us on the team heard. Demons dread being cast out of their homes. (Matthew 8:28-29) I am convinced, if we had not obeyed Jesus Christ and waited, we would have had absolute chaos in that auditorium. By insisting on silence I exerted my authority in Christ. When attendees complied, they took authority over the demons that were agitating them to keep talking and moving. If we had permitted that atmosphere, demons would have put on a dramatic show. Many people would have suffered as we expelled demons in Jesus's name. Our Holy Spirit is wonderful!

10) To take control of demons we have to obey God and take control of ourselves. Is there an area in your life where obeying God seems inconvenient or moves against people's expectations of you? What fruit could result from your obedience?

_____

_____

_____

_____

_____

_____

Bridge for Peace Foundation for Freedom

PRAYER FOR DELIVERANCE THROUGH JESUS CHRIST

Heavenly Father, I come to You in the name of Jesus. You are my Lord, I worship You alone. I am Your child. Today I recommit myself totally to You. Thank You Jesus Christ for the inheritance You have given me. You have paid the price for my salvation, healing, deliverance, and provision. You made Satan powerless and freed me. I treasure the inheritance You won for me. Thank You Holy Spirit, my Teacher, Counselor, and Comforter for living in me.

In the authority of the name of Jesus, Who disarmed the evil powers that ruled us and triumphed over demonic principalities and powers, I command every demonic power to be silent. I cut off all demonic communication. I thank You Lord for sending angels to guard us. I pray freedom through the power of the blood of Jesus Christ for all of us here.

Holy Spirit, thank You for bringing to our minds any need we have to repent. We acknowledge our sins, repent, and ask Your forgiveness. We thank You for cleansing us through the saving blood of Jesus Christ. Thank You Lord for restoring us to You. Through You, we will demonstrate good results of restoration as You produce evidence of Your love in our lives through Your power.

As we forgive those who have harmed us and pray for You to bless them, we thank You Lord for Your healing power released through our lives. You are eternal and present in all time right now. You remember what we have forgotten.

Thank You for healing all of our wounds. Thank You for healing us from any negative repercussions from wounds we have sustained. Thank You Lord, that You have told us to resist the Devil and he must go. We do resist the Devil in Your name. We receive the finished work You did for us at the cross.

I cancel every negative word spoken over us. I cancel all results of negative self-talk. I break every curse in the name of Jesus. Thank You Jesus that You became a curse for us and so we are free.

We present ourselves to You Lord, as living sacrifices, alive because of Your life in us. We have been made whole and acceptable to You through Jesus Christ. We will not be conformed to this world. Every demonic influence that we have accommodated, we reject now. Thank You that we have been transformed through Jesus Christ.

I enforce the power of the cross of Jesus Christ and command every evil spirit to go quietly now. As Jesus Christ's ambassador, I tear down every stronghold in us. Thank You Lord that You have given us a spirit of love, power, and a sound mind. You have not given us a spirit of fear. We reject all fear in the name of Jesus.

We cover ourselves in the saving blood of Jesus Christ and thank You, Holy Spirit, for bringing the completed work of the crucifixion into our lives today. Thank You that resurrection power is in us today. Thank You Lord that You have victory over every demonic spirit. We have the fullness of joy in You. We have new wine in You. We pray with gratitude in the name of Jesus Christ. Amen.

Answer Key

Chapter One

Inheritance

KEY TO UNDERSTANDING

1) Titus 3:4-7 "When God our Savior revealed his kindness and love, He saved us, not because of the righteous things we had done, but because of His mercy. He washed away our sins, giving us a new birth and new life through the Holy Spirit. He generously poured out the Spirit upon us through Jesus Christ our Savior. Because of His grace He made us right in His sight and gave us confidence that we will inherit eternal life."

2) Romans 10:13 "Everyone who calls on the name of the LORD will be saved."

3) Acts 15:11 "We believe that we are all saved the same way, by the undeserved grace of the Lord Jesus."

4) When we don't believe God has given us what we need we are open to many temptations. These can include fear, depression, self-pity, covetousness, cheating, thievery, and murder.

5) I have witnessed a shift in people as they grasp this life-changing truth.

6) 2Timothy 1:14 "Through the power of the Holy Spirit who lives within us, carefully guard the precious truth that has been entrusted to you."

7) I have noticed as I "spend" the inheritance Christ has won for me, I discover how it never runs out. As I use my inheritance in Christ, I begin to see how inexhaustible it is!

8) Through *Foundation for Freedom,* I have accessed more of what Jesus has for me in the area of deliverance. I am reminded of Christ's parable—to those who have more will be given. I know I have so much in Christ, but God keeps showing me it is more!

YOUR LEGACY

9)   Your Needs   Your Inheritance
          Resources as B4P grows   Provision

A Course in Deliverance

HOW DO I KNOW I WILL INHERIT IT?

10) Personal Answer

11) Reviewing His promises, recounting blessings already given, studying faithfulness scriptures.

12) Ephesians 1:11 "Furthermore, because we are united with Christ, we have received an inheritance from God, for He chose us in advance, and He makes everything work out according to His plan."

13) John 15:16 "You didn't choose Me. I chose you. I appointed you to go and produce lasting fruit, so that the Father will give you whatever you ask for, using My name."

14) Personal Answer

15) Ephesians 1:3-6 "All praise to God, the Father of our Lord Jesus Christ, Who has blessed us with every spiritual blessing in the heavenly realms because we are united with Christ. Even before He made the world, God loved us and chose us in Christ to be holy and without fault in His eyes. God decided in advance to adopt us into His own family by bringing us to Himself through Jesus Christ. This is what He wanted to do, and it gave Him great pleasure. So we praise God for the glorious grace He has poured out on us who belong to His dear Son."

GOD'S CHOICE IS NOT BASED ON OUR PERFORMANCE

16) Bible promise books that categorize scriptures under different headings are helpful. A concordance that lists words used in Scripture is also a good tool. I might study scriptures that teach about God to understand who I am. I might look up scriptures that reveal how everything depends on God.

ADOPTION

17) Meditating on these truths moves me to worship and increases my gratitude.

THE LANGUAGE OF THE CROSS

18) The blood of Jesus.

19) Reviewing the history of sacrifices that were inadequate causes me to celebrate Jesus and that I am living in the days of the New Covenant.

20) I can best use what God has given to me by obeying Him.

Chapter Two

Strongholds

TEACHABLE

1) Gamaliel had more experience than Saul. That could account for his wait-and-see attitude. Gamaliel had more political savvy than Saul. Some think he may have believed Jesus was the Messiah. Gamaliel would have known how to achieve his own ends without risk to himself. He may have tried to offer some protection to Christ's followers without exposing himself to condemnation.

2) Thank You Lord for all who have helped me to know You. Holy Spirit please correct any teachings I have accepted that are not true. Thank you Jesus for delivering me from any confusion in my mind about Your nature, Word, or expectations. I want to receive everything You have for me and live for You. Amen.

CHANGE IN PLANS

3) Before Ed resigned, we prayed together. We agreed that God was leading us in a new direction. Then God sent me a very vivid dream, which we both accepted as our answer. Temptations continued to surface, but as we sought answers from God we came to know Him better. We learned so much from the Holy Spirit through the experience.

CHANGE OF HEART

4) Philippians 2:9-11 "Therefore, God elevated Him to the place of highest honor and gave Him the name above all other names, that at the name of Jesus every knee should bow, in heaven and on earth and under the earth, and every tongue declare that Jesus Christ is Lord, to the glory of God the Father."

5) Ananias laid his hands on Saul. He told Saul he had been sent by God so that Saul could get his sight back and be filled with the Holy Spirit.

6) I recommit myself to serve Christ and to be free of every resistance or reluctance through the power of His blood.

Answer Key

A Course in Deliverance

EQUIPPING

7) Do not leave Jerusalem until the Father sends you what He promised. You will be baptized with the Holy Spirit.

8) Supernatural sound, wind, and fire appeared. They started speaking in other languages.

9) Jesus knew people need His power to fulfill His mission.

THE BATTLEFIELD

10) Paul describes strongholds as belonging to the Devil and keeping people from knowing God. A stronghold is like a wall that blocks the truth. Paul says our spiritual weapons are a mighty arsenal that pulls strongholds down.

11) Ananias had a stronghold of fear and prejudice that caused him to question God and resist His purpose. Ananias could have missed his call, but he submitted to God. If I judge others it is disobedience, and that is dangerous. I need the Holy Spirit to alert me to prejudices.

12) Personal answer.

13) Scripture tells us never to think more highly of ourselves than of others. That is a good weapon for combating prejudice. Transparency is a great weapon against the enemy. Repentance is powerful. Keeping relationships straight fosters community. When people see Christian unity and experience Christian love, freedom results.

14) Father, thank You for Your plans to make us one. I reject every prejudice I have inherited through my family line, workplace, nation, and any other source. I thank You for using me to minister to all people as You see fit. And I welcome Your plan for my life. Amen.

15) Everywhere! I thank God He has supplied it and shows me that I have free access to His power through Jesus Christ.

Chapter Three

Take the Snake By the Tail

DELIVERANCE AND DESTINY

1) Destruction of newborn boys by the ruling authority occurred after Moses and Jesus were born. The wisdom and action of Moses's mother saved him. The wisdom and action of Jesus's step-father saved His life.

2) Yes, in America there is widespread destruction of unborn children. Government representatives have passed laws that permit children to undergo abortion without their parents' knowledge. Prayer, giving, and political activism are ways we participate in the spiritual battle.

3) For I know the plans I have for Annette. They are plans for good and not for disaster, to give Annette a future and a hope.

4) Personal answer.

DISCOVER STRENGTH

5) Personal answer.

MEET RESISTANCE WITH CONFINDENCE IN THE LORD

6) Personal answer.

7) Personal answer.

8) Personal answer.

9) Personal answer.

MASTER YOUR WILLPOWER TO SEE GOD'S POWER

10) Personal answer.

11) Personal answer.

Answer Key

Chapter Four

Authority

1) There is freedom for us all from spirits of fear through God's Word and the power of Christ.

2) Jesus told the demon to be silent and to come out of the man.

AUTHORITY AND POWER

3) All power has been given to Jesus Christ. We have been given authority to teach God's Word.

4) Satan will be driven out. Christ has judged him. He has no power over Jesus.

5) Personal answer.

TERRITORIAL SPIRITS

6) Daniel showed perseverance that led to an amazing visitation and revelation that I benefit from today.

7) Personal answer.

8) Personal answer.

9) Personal answer.

CULTIVATING AN AWARENESS OF GOD

10) Personal answer.

11) Personal answer.

SNAKE-FREE ZONE

12) I've participated in the Snake-Free Zone all over the world and it is always powerful.

Chapter Five

Rule Over Rebellion

REBELLION

1) Moses prayed and then rebuked the rebels. He warned them, which gave them an opportunity to consider their actions and repent.

BEARING FRUIT

2) Jesus tells us He has chosen us and appointed us. He tells us to go and bear fruit that will last. Lasting fruit is produced through us by the Holy Spirit as we obey Jesus's commands.

3) Noticing the vulnerable area helps me to realize "foxes" are prowling around. Praying for wisdom keeps me alert. The blood of Jesus and the authority of His name expel demons.

PERSEVERANCE

4) My CD *In the Secret Place* explores abiding in Christ in greater depth.

BREAKING CURSES

5) Personal answer.

6) Personal answer.

A HOLY DEMAND

7) Personal answer.

8) Personal answer.

DELIVERED FROM WITCHCRAFT

9) Staying close to the Word of God that says we have been made righteous through Christ's crucifixion. Relying on wisdom through the Holy Spirit, and not the reason of man, safeguards us.

Answer Key

A Course in Deliverance

Chapter Six

The Piercing Sword

THE SWORD OF THE SPIRIT PIERCES

1) The armor of God includes the belt of truth, breastplate of righteousness, shoes on your feet—the eagerness to spread the gospel of peace, and the shield of faith to stop the burning arrows of the Evil One. The helmet of salvation and the sword of the Spirit, the Word of God complete the armor. Personal answer for your interpretation of the use of the armor.

2) Personal answer.

3) God's Word is living, active, sharper than any known swords. It penetrates unseen places, and discerns the reflections and the thoughts of the heart.

GOD'S WORD IS FULL OF LIVING POWER

4) Personal answer.

CUT THROUGH DECEPTION

5) Personal answer.

6) The Lord will annihilate Satan.

7) Personal answer.

8) To think that God would make us as His very own mouth if we distinguish the precious from the base, the holy from the common, is both awe inspiring and compelling!

9) God is always willing to help at every moment. And He is able.

SMOKE AND MIRRORS

10) Personal answer.

11) Paul tells us those who dispute the truth are trapped by the devil. He counsels us to correct and instruct them gently that the Holy Spirit might free them to see God's truth.

12) Jesus has called and equipped us for the task.

Chapter Seven

Choose Life

WE NEED OUR SAVIOR

1) God is the living God, Savior of all. We are to teach this.

2) Personal answer.

AGREEMENT AND UNITY

3) Life is good when unity abounds. It is precious and to be treasured, it is refreshing and produces growth like dew in the lands. God's blessing will be upon a united team. A team that fits this description will move as one under God's direction. Satan thrives on fear and chaos, the opposite of unity. When we submit to God, His anointing on our team is visible. When we do not hinder Him He moves swiftly through us to set the captive free.

HIGH ABOVE OUR WAYS

4) Personal answer.

JESUS THE TRUE FRIEND

5) Personal answer.

UNMASKED

6) Scriptural truth exposes lies and penetrates the darkness.

THE STILL SMALL VOICE

7) Looking into the mirror of God's Word we grow bold as we see His holiness and His might. Reading His Word is excellent preparation. Consider meditating on a particular verse that captures your attention. Perhaps you would want to memorize something that you read.

8) In the Bible Jesus demonstrated how to deliver people from Satan. He wants everyone to walk confidently in God. He made it simple. Let us imitate Him.

9) Personal answer.

Answer Key

A Course in Deliverance

Chapter Eight

Delivered

VULNERABLE

1) Unaware of our preciousness, we may yield when we should stand firm.

2) Identifying susceptible areas is, in itself, a safeguard against temptation.

DETERMINED

3) Esau took his inheritance for granted. Naboth valued his inheritance. His actions showed he had thought it through, felt the blessing and responsibility of what he had been given. He guarded it with determination.

THE HEIR

4) Personal answer.

RESSURECTION POWER

5) Look closely at the premise Satan proposes and you will find deception.

6) Christ had memorized Scripture and answered Satan with verses. Christ introduced each verse with, "It is said...." These introductions were the only words Christ spoke to Satan that were not Scripture. Satan had also memorized Scripture. He twisted the meaning to suit his own ends. Christ not only knew the Scripture, but He had discerned the intended meaning.

7) Realizing suicide is a spirit empowers and equips.

8) Receiving Christ, scriptural truth, testimonies, sometimes repentance, receiving forgiveness and knowing sin is washed away by Christ all can break spirits of shame.

FROM DEATH TO LIFE

9) Jesus wrecked the plans of the demonic hierarchy. He made a show of them as captives. It is a great image that reflects an amazing truth.

THE DAY THE DEMONS SHRIEKED

10) Last night a young woman told me how hard it can be to move against the expectations of the world. She named it "fear of man." I discussed with her how Satan exerts greater pressure when we are about to bear fruit. Obedience to God always brings imperishable fruit that remains for eternity—the fruit Jesus commanded from our lives.

Foundation for Healing Bible Course and Companion DVD

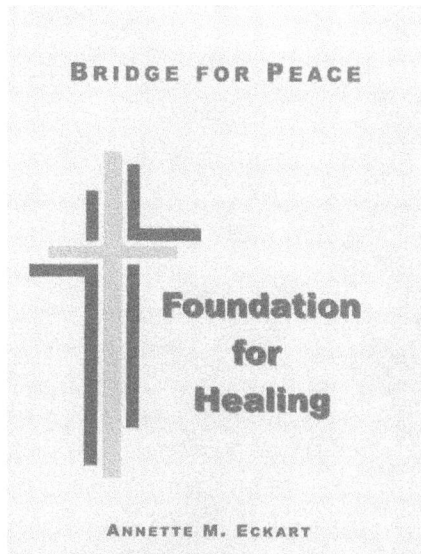

BRIDGE FOR PEACE

Foundation for Healing

ANNETTE M. ECKART

Foundation for Healing Bible Course is the fruit of 20 years of Annette Eckart's ministering healing in the name of Jesus Christ. Learn and grow as you respond to questions that explore Scripture and invite you to reflect on your experience. Read about miracles today in this 12 week course.

Foundation for Healing Companion DVD

is conveniently divided into 12 titles that can be shown weekly. Each title has 20 minutes of Annette Eckart's dynamic teaching. This DVD is an invaluable tool to maximize your study experience.

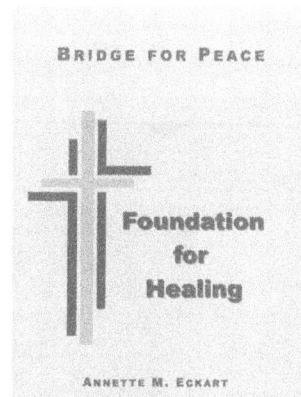

BRIDGE FOR PEACE

Foundation for Healing

ANNETTE M. ECKART

To order: **Foundation for Healing** Bible Course *and DVD or other resources visit our Website www.bridgeforpeace.org or Call 1.631.730.3982*

WAKE UP

Annette M. Eckart

Wake Up!

Discover who you are in

Jesus Christ

Annette shares stories of defining moments for biblical heroes. They woke up to realize God's marvelous deeds. Wake up from the hypnotic spell of Satan that has persuaded you in the past. Don't let Satan tell you who you are! Wake up and receive Holy Spirit empowerment for your great God-given purpose. Annette helps you realize that you walk under an open heaven, you are a memorial stone with feet and you are a spiritual heir.

When stressed and oppressed you need COURAGE!

Annette teaches you how to claim COURAGE through Jesus Christ

COURAGE

Annette M. Eckart

Prepare a space to contain the blessings God will pour in. Humorous and touching testimonies, healing reports, and Annette's experience of Holy Spirit visions and God-given dreams will encourage you. She talks about hearing God's voice with specific examples that will energize you to *Dig in with God.*

Annette helps you to:

- Recognize God's voice

- Believe for the work He is doing in you

- Reap the rewards of faith

Annette M. Eckart

DIG IN with GOD

www.ingramcontent.com/pod-product-compliance
Lightning Source LLC
Chambersburg PA
CBHW062103090426

42741CB00015B/3313